Battleground Europe
POLYGON WOOD

Battleground Europe

POLYGON WOOD

Nigel Cave

Series editor
Nigel Cave

LEO COOPER

First published in 1999 by
LEO COOPER
an imprint of
Pen Sword Books Limited
47 Church Street, Barnsley, South Yorkshire S70 2AS

ISBN 0 85052 606 X

A CIP catalogue of this book is available
from the British Library

Printed by Redwood Books Limited
Trowbridge, Wiltshire

For up-to-date information on other titles produced under the Leo Cooper imprint,
please telephone or write to:
Pen & Sword Books Ltd, FREEPOST, 47 Church Street
Barnsley, South Yorkshire S70 2AS
Telephone 01226 734222

CONTENTS

A panorama taken from Polygon Wood looking towards Zonnebeke, showing Australians troops occupying shell holes, 21 September, 1917.

Acknowledgements

The book has relied heavily on the work of the authors of the Official Historians, most notably that of the great Hertford Historian C.E.W. Bean and his team. The Australian Official History is a quite extraordinary document and provides a great wealth of information. The histories of the 7th and 23rd Divisions have also been most helpful. I would like to place on record my grateful thanks to various survivors of 110 (Leicesters) Brigade, whose anecdotal accounts have contributed significantly to the text. The Public Record Office at Kew is a mine of information, and the staff there are tremendously helpful and patient. This is a very user-friendly archive, and anyone interested in the Great War should not be daunted by the sheer bulk of the material and the seeming complexity of the system.

I would like to express my thanks to the various landowners around Polygon Wood, who were helpful both in matters of access and in providing local information.

I would also like to take this opportunity once more of thanking Tony Spagnoly who years ago shared his enthusiasm for the battlefields and his 'on the ground approach' with me. I would strongly recommend readers to invest in his (and Ted Smith's) range of publications (also under the Leo Cooper, Pen and Sword imprint), volumes such as *Salient Points I and II* and *A Walk Around Plugstreet;* and the earlier *Anatomy of a Raid,* now available in the same style as the others in stiff back format.

Richard Brucciani once more flew me over this part of the Battlefields; we enjoyed two gloriously sunny days in September 1997 flying up and down the front lines in the Ypres area.

The work on the ground for this book was done in the winter months of 1998/99. The weather for it was surprisingly good, and certainly excellent for touring the battlefield. I would like to thank Dan and James Saunders who accompanied me on these trips and who proved adept at exploring the depths of Polygon Wood in search of bunkers, whilst I stood on the rides waiting for a specific point to which I could fight my way.

The staff at Pen and Sword have now got all my foibles to a tee and still manage to produce what I like to think is a reasonable end result; for that much of the credit must go to Paul and Roni Wilkinson.

The CWGC have once again been most helpful, lending the relevant registers at a modest charge. The work they do is of great significance for all of us, but especially to those who travel to France and Belgium frequently to study the battlefields.

Introduction

Polygon Wood 1917 is a story of some of the events that took part in the wood and its immediate surroundings in the autumn of 1917. It makes no attempt to be comprehensive and does not cover any of the events of 1914 or in the spring of 1915, which I hope will be the subject of a separate book. To include them in this work could lead to confusion, especially as the line was going in the opposite direction to that in 1917!

It has always been a rather special place for me; it remains a quiet part of the Salient, in contrast to the quite rapid developments that have taken place since my first visit here in 1968. I find it an area that allows for walking and looking and thinking without being too conscious of the reality of the world of 1999. Although the landscape bears no resemblance to the ferocious scenes that scarred it in late 1917, it is a good place in which to reflect on the gruesome past. I am not one to ponder on the futility of the Great War; I happen to think that there were great issues at stake, probably worth fighting for even in the context of today's standards. The 'futility' of the Great War, to my mind, has far more to do with post-war events than with what happened during it; though obviously actions (or lack of actions) are open to informed criticism.

The Battle of Third Ypres is probably the most misunderstood of all the battles of the Great War in British experience; though the Somme must come a close second, with the seeming impossibility of getting the common perception to move on from 1 July 1916. Certainly there were times when Third Ypres degenerated into a slog of tragic proportions in a dismal landscape, sodden with water and bogged down in mud. Human suffering existed on a grand scale. But significant chunks of the battle were fought in good, sunny weather; the dust was a frequent cause for complaint throughout September. There were notable tactical gains; whilst the fighting methods of the British army continued to develop at notable speed. Many of those who were participants in both battles considered the conditions in the latter stages of the Somme worse than anything that Third Ypres threw up; and of course the casualties on the Somme were far greater than Third Ypres. What is sure is that Third Ypres was fought in the third year of the war – is there no end? – whilst the gains made so painstakingly were lost so rapidly in April 1918. Less commonly mentioned is how even more rapidly they were retaken in the autumn of 1918.

And then there is the common British fault of seeing everything from that perspective – little consideration seems to be given to the impact of the battle upon the German army.

It is my hope that this series of guides will continue to encourage people to delve further and understand why things happened; all too often we know the outcome but not necessarily the context in which it occurred. Perhaps the most useful things these guides do is to encourage people to get out on to the ground, because this is where the battles were actually ought, and the topography explains much. At the risk of looking slightly ludicrous (and I am sure many of the locals think we are all mad in any case!) crouch down and try and see things from the viewpoint of the trench level – it does make a very noticeable difference.

Polygon Wood is a special place for me too because of my grandfather's experience here in October 1917; and it was at Polygon Wood that the Kitchener battalions of the Leicestershire Regiment won their VC. The Buttes cemetery in the early hours, or as sun sets, is a beautiful and meditative place; I hope others will be introduced, now, to this experience.

Nigel Cave
Ratcliffe College, Leicestershire.

Dedication.

This book is dedicated to the memory of Mike Lyddiard, Director of Toc H, who died very suddenly in Poperinge in March 1999. An army career was cut short by a severe rugby injury; thereafter he worked for people. This took him from the Children's Society to UNICEF and, finally, to Toc H.

Mike was deeply touched by the Great War and took much pleasure from regular, quite long, stays at Talbot House. He was moved by his time in the Salient to write some poems and reflections, published in *Only Remembered*. Polygon Wood is described in this work in a chapter entitled *A Place of Peace*. It seems right to dedicate this work to Mike, a delightful and unobtrusive gentleman, a loving husband to his wife Ruth and father of Rachel and James, who has done so much in recent years to keep one great heritage of World War One functioning efficiently and effectively, Tubby Clayton's beloved Toc H.

8

Advice for Tourers

Ypres (or Ieper as it is known in Belgium and, perhaps more importantly, as it is signposted) is very close to Calais or the Shuttle terminus - about a 75 minute journey from the former and a few minutes longer from the latter. Simply follow the signs to Dunkerque (Dunkirk) on the new(ish) motorway and then follow them to Ypres (marked off this road) which brings you to the A25. Come off at the junction (number 13) marked Steenvoorde and Ypres (Ieper); turn left and cross into Belgium after a few miles, and then it is plain sailing to a place whose name resonated around the world between 1914 and 1918.

There are numerous places to stay in Ypres and in the surrounding area - a full list may be obtained from the Tourist Office in the Cloth Hall: Dienst Toerisme Ieper, Stadhuis, Grote Markt 8900 IEPER. Tel: +32 57 20 07 24; Fax +32 57 21 85 89. There is a British run B & B in

View of Ypres from the ramparts in the immediate post war period.
TAYLOR LIBRARY

Ypres in happier, pre-war times. Notice that St Martins now has a full sized spire.

Ypres itself, 'The Shell Hole', D'Hondstraat 54 - 58, 8900 IEPER, Tel +32 57 20 87 58. This has the added advantage of being co-located with the proprietor's (John Woolsgrove) excellent bookshop - new and second hand - and where you may also purchase a vast array of equipment, uniform etc from the period. Another place worth considering is Talbot House in Poperinge, the original Toc H. It offers

basic rooms holding from one to four people and has self catering facilities. Contact Talbot House, Gaasthuisstraat 43, 8970 POPERINGE, Tel +32 57 33 32 28. Closer to Polygon Wood is the hotel in the rebuilt Hooge Chateau - though the new one was built some distance from the original. Kasteelhof 't Hooghe, Meenseweg 481, 8902 IEPER, Tel/Fax +32 57 46 87 87. It has the added advantage in that the crater in the hotel grounds was the location of various headquarters during the battles in Polygon Wood, and a high proportion of the soldiers involved in the story in this book would have passed through, or close to, the grounds. There is also a B & B, which

Aerial view of Ypres today, looking westwards.

has been recommended to me by friends who have stayed there, a little further to the east: The Protea B & B, 47 Menenstraat, 8980 Geluveld-Zonnebeke. The rooms are en suite and with TV. Tel + 32 57 46 63 39; Fax +32 57 46 63 98.

There are a variety of museums for you to visit whilst here. The 'In Flanders Fields' museum in the Cloth Hall is a new, high-tech affair, somewhat controversial, but nevertheless interesting whatever your personal views might be. It takes a considerable time to view properly, and I would urge a visit either early on in the day or towards the end of the afternoon - this advice particularly relevant during UK school term time, when the hordes of British youth descend upon the place. To get some idea about the trenches, to view quite horrifying stereoscopic

ROAD TO VLAMERTINGE

The awesome display of shells in the Hooge Chapel Museum.

One of the museum's tableaux showing a German signaller at work.

pictures and to see a wonderful range of headgear from the early days of the war, then Sanctuary Wood/Hill 62 Museum is the place for you, well signposted off the Menin Road, up Canadalaan. This is the oldest continuously run museum (the Second World War apart) in the Salient, opening in the early 1920s. Again, it gets very busy, but early morning visits can normally be made in peace and quiet. The Hooge Chapel Museum is housed in the former small chapel, opposite Hooge Crater Military Cemetery. As well as offering light snacks and a comfortable drinks area, the museum is very well presented with effectively recreated scenes and some fascinating displays, not least the vast array of shells in the old entrance. Another excellent museum is that housed in the chateau at Zonnebeke, near the church in the centre of the village. It has variable opening hours (times from the local tourist office or from the information board near Tyne Cot Cemetery), but is an eloquent testimonial to the impact of war on a large village which found itself in the middle of heavy fighting in the second stage of Third Ypres.

The tours in this section can probably be done in the course of a long day, but it would be preferable to do it over a couple of days. There are a number of restaurants and cafes near Polygon Wood itself, a popular walking area and now a nature reserve. The roads round and about the wood are narrow, barely allowing two cars to pass, and there are a number of very sharp bends in the road, so more than average care needs to be taken both in driving or in leaving your car in a place that will not obstruct traffic.

The best time to visit the area is in late autumn and then through to the early spring - the crops will not be high in the fields and the vegetation in the wood will have died down, though the wood has few deciduous trees (as was the case in 1914) and retains a certain gloom and melancholy all year round. It is best to take walking boots with you, as the tracks are nearly all muddy, and parts of Polygon Wood, especially on the east side where the Polygonebeek rises, can be very marshy - and often, indeed, flooded.

Please take all the normal precautions for insurance. A Green Card is almost certainly no longer required (but this can vary between insurance companies, so check); and an E1 11 form (obtainable from main post offices) gives reciprocal health cover, though this is not as all-encompassing in some respects as that on offer from the NHS. It is advisable to take out personal insurance and vehicle cover in case of breakdown. Motorists should have at least one warning triangle, though two are sometimes required, and a basic First Aid Kit, as well

Polygon Wood looking to the south west.

as essential spares. When walking some form of headgear would be sensible, a waterproof, a compass, camera and spare battery and films, a notebook and pencil, a bottle opener and corkscrew, a couple of mugs and a bread knife. There are plenty of supermarkets around from which to purchase the makings of a picnic; there is a good one opposite St Martin's Church in the centre of Ypres.

Eating in the evening - or any other time, for that matter - poses no problem, with a full range of restaurants on the square. Restaurants are quite happy to arrange your meal around the Last Post ceremony at the Menin Gate, which takes place at 8 pm each evening.

The maps in this book are adequate for your purposes, but you might wish to purchase the relevant Blue series (1:25000) map, 28/3-4 Geluveld-Moorsele, at the tourist office in Ypres. The French Green series (1:100000) No 2 Lille-Dunkerque is excellent for navigation purposes. For those who are members of the Western Front Association there is a trench map service. The most relevant one is 28 NE 3, Gheluvelt. Details about the Association and membership may be obtained from: The Western Front Association, PO Box 1914, Reading, Berks. RG4 7YP.

There are a number of general guides to the Salient - the most recent of these is *Walking the Salient* by Paul Reed, whilst Major and Mrs Holts *Battlefield Guide*, Ypres Salient is both very full and is accompanied by an excellent map. There are several guides to sections of the Salient published in the *Battleground Europe* series; whilst John Giles', *Flanders Then and Now* is still available, with its mixture of war time and contemporary photographs (though these are being overtaken by the rapid development of the area) and accompanying explanatory text, often from soldiers of the time. Finally, there is Rose Coombs' *Before Endeavours Fade,* the well-established vade mecum to the battlefields, which gives an excellent coverage of the memorials and cemeteries of the Western Front, but most particularly of the British sector.

Third Ypres is a battle that has inspired almost as much polemical writing as the First Battle of the Somme. Lyn Macdonald's *They Called it Passchendaele* is based heavily on veterans' recollections and is available in paperback. Also still in print is the controversial efforts of Leon Wolff, *In Flanders Fields*; whilst Prior and Wilson have written *Passchendaele: the Untold Story.* It seems to me that the definitive book of this battle has yet to be written - especially one that takes into greater account the other half of the story, that is the German perspective.

The Ypres salient can be a complicated battlefield to understand, and it would help (though it is not essential) if time was spent getting to know the topography of the area. The battlefield around Polygon Wood does suffer from one major change in the physical setting since the war, and that is the construction of the A19 motorway that cuts a swathe to the south west of the wood, distorting the landscape with its cutting. That very significant factor apart, this is a quiet part of the battlefield, the eastern part of which is rarely explored. Most visitors will come and see the two cemeteries either in or adjacent to the wood on its northern side; a visit to the Buttes Military Cemetery in the evening or early morning is, to my mind, especially moving.

Details of burials may be obtained from the Commonwealth War Graves Commission. They have an office where traces can be made in Elverdingestraat 82, which is several hundred yards further along the road from St George's Memorial Church. The registers for the two cemeteries at Polygon Wood are often missing - those for the Buttes and the New Zealand Memorial have, indeed, been permanently removed and have to be inspected at the office in Ypres. The reason for this would seem to be local vandalism - they were removed long before the unhappy trait began a few years ago of stealing registers from cemeteries.

Munitions and other dangerous relics of the war are not as common in the Salient as they are on other parts of the battlefield, but they do exist and they are all potentially lethal. Please just leave them alone. I am certain that there is legislation or by-laws that forbid the use of

metal detectors and digging in Polygon Wood itself, and everything else is private property. It would be a sensible precaution to ensure that your tetanus jab is up to date – rusty metal is dangerous at the best of times, but when one considers the bodies that were (are) in the ground and the types of gas and high explosive shells that poured into the area, the risk is all that much greater.

These grenades and shells still kill! Look but please leave them alone.

17

A note about Trench Maps.

Those used in this book are based on a scale of 1:10000; when there were was a period when the line moved frequently, as in the case for Polygon Wood in 1917, these maps were updated on a regular, almost weekly, basis. Many of the extracts from the trench maps used in this book come from one dated (or rather corrected) as 14.9.17. The sheet number is 28 NE 3, Gheluvelt.

The map is subdivided into numbered squares, running from 1 – 36, running in six lines, 1 - 6. 7 – 12 etc, covering an area 6,000 yards by 6,000 yards; this large area was given a letter of the alphabet to identify it, and in this book we are exclusively concerned with J. Each numbered square covered an area 1,000 yards by 1,000 yards. Each numbered square in turn was subdivided into four smaller squares, known, clockwise, as a, b, d, c. These in turn could be subdivided by using small lines marking 50 yard intervals on both the northing and the easting. Thus it was possible to give very accurate references. An example of a reference would be J.10.a.6.8 for the mound in Polygon Wood. Always use the easting number first (ie the bottom line) followed by the northing number.

Maps

Chapter One

THE CAPTURE OF POLYGON WOOD
26 SEPTEMBER 1917

Prelude: 20 September 1917

One of the determining factors in the geographical boundaries laid down for this book has been the construction of the A19 motorway, running to the south west of Polygon Wood. This makes it quite difficult to follow on the ground the various movements of the troops, so it has been decided that this part of the action will be included in a later work on the Battle of the Menin Road.

What undoubtedly has been lost to most people in the persistence of the association of Third Ypres with the village of Passchendaele and rain, mud, more mud and desolation, are the considerable developments in a whole range of areas in both the offensive and the defensive. In the offensive there was further work on the artillery, the use of wireless, continued progress in the matter of logistics,

Fatigue party (in more ways than one) during the Third Battle of Ypres.

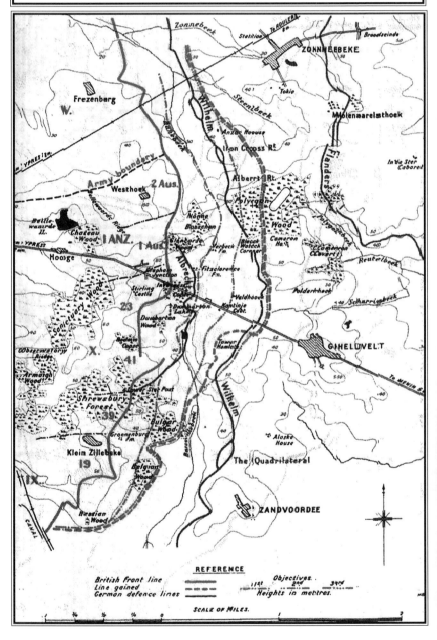

developing battalion, company, platoon and section formations and tactics - and so it continues. In the defence there was further experimentation with the idea of counter-attack (or *Eingreif*) divisions and the use of low-flying aircraft. There were also a number of limited, bite and hold, offensives which were extremely successful - and this applies to both the Battle of the Menin Road and the Battle of Polygon Wood. The weather was full of contrasts - whereas August was a month notable for the quite appalling and unusual level of rainfall, September was very dry. So, undoubtedly, conditions were absolutely abysmal for much of the battle, especially at its beginning and in the final weeks, and the landscape was transformed from what is actually pretty bleak most of the time into utter devastation. Yet the Third Battle of Ypres was also vitally important in the continuing evolution and development of both armies, British and German.

The offensive came to a temporary halt on 28 August, and Plumer's Second Army moved into the southern half of the Salient to take over the offensive there, heading for the Gheluvelt Plateau; as the battle progressed his left extended further and further to the left, taking on the responsibility for capturing the Broodseinde Ridge and Passchendaele, securing the right flank whilst Gough's Fifth Army worked its way north eastwards.

The Official History summarises the situation at the end of August,

The casualties alone (68,100 from 31 July - 28 August) do not give the full picture of the situation; for, apart from actual losses, the discomfort of the living conditions in the forward areas and the strain of fighting with indifferent success had overwrought and discouraged all ranks more than any other operation fought by British troops in the War, so that, although the health of the troops did not suffer, discontent was general: the soldier hates discomfort more than he fears danger.[1]

What a contrast this comment is to that which the Official Australian Historian makes of the atmosphere on the late morning of 20 September.

It is difficult to recapture the sudden lift of spirits experienced throughout the British side on that battlefield when news spread that the British line again ran across the main heights, through Polygon Wood.

He goes on to say

This success differed from all others in which Australians had yet participated, in that it was part of a well planned series of operations leading definitely towards victory in the war. But,

though it caused some rejoicing in England and France, its real importance was probably underrated there; earlier failures had caused the people to be cautious and the governments sceptical.[2]

Plumer was given three weeks to prepare his Army for the next phase of the battle. The preparations were extraordinarily methodical and massive in their scale; the main purpose of these efforts was to bring up the artillery, build emplacements and provide the infrastructure to maintain the vast quantities of ammunition that these guns would require. The two main railheads for the supply of ammunition between them could only take a maximum of eleven trains a day, and it was estimated that his plans required 156 trainloads above normal usage. Light railways were laid to bring material up from here closer to the line.

The roads were also a major problem. One way circuits were built, for example at Hooge, made for the most part of planks. This process was assisted by the dry weather, '...the sea of mud in the forward area gradually turned into a brown dusty desert'.[3] I Anzac required eighty motor lorries each day, each carrying three tons of planks from Ouderdom railway siding, through Ypres and up the Menin Road to Birr Cross. Once these lorries were clear of Ypres on their return journey a hundred and twenty two horse wagons drove out from the town to these roadside dumps and took the planks forward to the work parties (some of whom were amongst the 12,500 Labour Corps and a thousand from the British West Indies Regiment working in the Second Army area). The road circuits were completed on 19 September just before the assault was to be launched.[4]

The artillery plan was meticulously carried out - something that had become a feature of British assaults, at least in the opening phase of a battle, such as at Arras and Messines. However the long pause confused the Germans, who became convinced that the British were

General Herbert Plummer

moving their effort further south, something that might have been reinforced by the earlier attack, in mid August, of the Canadian Corps against Lens. The Germans became accustomed to a variable barrage, at different times of the day, of different length, and with a variety of ammunition. They appreciated a major attack was imminent as zero came closer, and captured documents from an officer in the early hours of 20 September confirmed this - but rather too late for them to put in an effective artillery protective blanket of their own.

At 5.40 am the British barrage came crashing down (although there had been a last minute panic, when rain threatened to question the timing of the operation); the counter batteries drenched the German batteries with gas shells. The men followed closely the creeping barrage (a line of artillery fire, designed to go forward in a sequence of timed lifts, behind which the infantry could advance and which kept the enemy under cover until the attackers were almost upon them); combined with the ground mist the British infantry appeared amongst the defenders, as one German put it, 'like spectres out of the mist'.

For the purposes of this book, the chief concern lies with the progress of the 1st Australian Division. Glencorse Wood and Nonne Boschen were taken quite smoothly. Resistance in a sunken road at the northern side of Glencorse Wood caused a temporary hold-up. A pillbox position had a German light machine-gun on top of it, and held

Burst of a German shell, part of a barrage, in the area of the advance sends at least two soldiers scurrying for safety.

up progress. Lieutenant GH Leaver was sent with his specially trained platoon to get around the position; he was within a few yards of the machine-gun when

> *one of the enemy with a revolver shot him through the head.* [Leaver is buried at Hooge Crater.] *The men went mad. A corporal of the 11th named Hodge rushed forward, shot the machine-gunner and overturned the gun. As the Australians swarmed into the road the Germans tried to surrender, but the excited troops 'filled the place with bombs' until, growing tired of killing, they allowed a remnant - an officer and 40 men - to go to the rear as prisoners.*[5]

The ground covered by much of the attack had already been won and lost on two previous occasions by British troops during August. Nonne Boschen (which is rapidly filling up with holiday homes, chalets and caravans), by then merely a waste, was crossed by keeping to the lips of the water-filled craters. The OH notes that a photograph taken on 1 October 1917 shows

> *a bare broken surface, like that of a slightly rough sea, with a number of hard, sharp-cut, water-filled craters; the wrecks of a few pillboxes are shown, but only two skeleton trees - even the stumps of the others have disappeared.*[6]

The western edge of Polygon Wood, the second objective, was reduced to a few saplings amongst an array of shell craters; this was achieved at about 7.45 am - up to the timetable.

To the left the 2nd Australian Division took the Wilhelm Line, which included the capture of three German strong points: Anzac

A line of concrete shelters in the swamp of Nonne Bosschen, taken by the 1st Australian Division on September 20th, showing the condition of the depressions on the battlefield even after several weeks of dry weather.

House, with a two storied observation bunker, had two large lower rooms and a smaller upper room, reached by a ladder. 15 Germans were captured as they were overpowered as they dragged a couple of machine-guns out into the open; and a field wireless was found installed in the upper room, with its loop holes for observation over the British line. Also to fall, further to the right, were the formidable redoubts at Iron Cross and Albert. These all formed part of the Wilhelm Line. Further to the left was another redoubt in this line. A part of the Bremen Redoubt was uncovered ten years or so ago in the large brick factory on the western outskirts of Zonnebeke and provides an interesting insight into the type of reinforced, underground accommodation provided for the defenders. Perhaps it was relatively secure, but the conditions inside can have been far from comfortable. The Bremen Redoubt can be viewed, but access is (at the time of

The two storied Anzac pillbox captured on 20 September 1917.

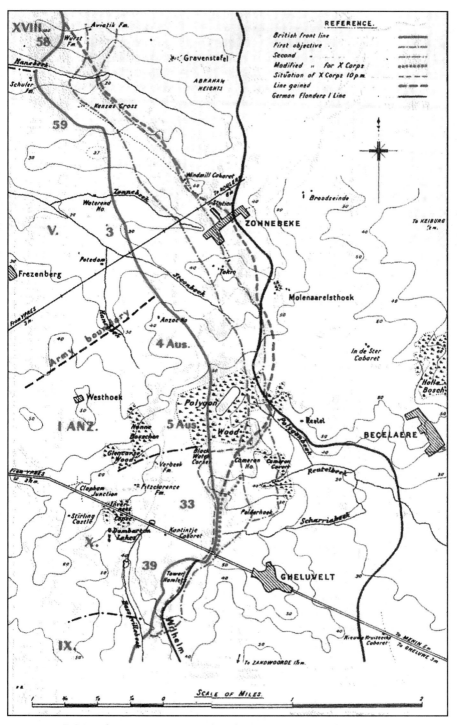

MAP 2: BATTLE OF 26 SEPTEMBER 1917

writing) usually only possible for groups and via the tourist office in Zonnebeke.

There was a halt on the second objective, mainly for the artillery to reorganise, but also for the infantry units as well. The loss of Anzac House deprived the Germans of their main artillery observation point over the Steenbeek valley to the north; some tidying up was done to remove hostile fire from Garter Point (a couple of hundred yards east of Anzac House) and from a strongpoint at Black Watch Corner, at the south western edge of Polygon Wood.

The advance to the third objective met little difficulty on the left, but on the right, to the south of Polygon Wood, things were rather more troublesome.

The Germans were at this stage unsure as to how far the British had advanced, The script called for the Germans to launch counter-attacks before the enemy could secure and consolidate their gains; an attempt early in the afternoon was foiled by the artillery acting under the

Detached groups of the 7th Australian Brigade manning shell holes and unconnected trenches, then the newly adopted method of minimizing the effect of German barrages. Polygon Wood, 21st September 1917.

observation of the several RFC squadrons operating over the battlefield. At just after 7 pm the British barrage came down on a body of Germans advancing up the Reutelbeek valley against the 23rd and 1st Australian Divisions.

At 7.02 pm, just when the moment for action seemed to have arrived, an intense barrage by field artillery and machine-guns, in answer to an SOS call, descended on the Germans gathering a few hundred yards away, the artillery barrage within half a minute of the signal, the machine-gun barrage within a few seconds. For forty to sixty minutes the area in front of both divisions was combed and recombed by fire, and the result was devastating. For the infantry awaiting the onslaught the reaction to this fire success was one of disappointment. An Australian officer, however, said afterwards that his men, south of Polygon Wood, simply sat back and laughed when they saw the opportunity they had been praying for snatched away at the last moment by the guns: they knew that the Germans would be unable to pass through such a barrage, and in fact no further sign of movement was seen that evening.[7]

Laying new light railway track close to the Front.

The German Spoiling Attack: 25 September 1917.

Plumer now needed a few days to bring his artillery forward; to do that light railways and plank roads had to be constructed, and this operation was assisted by fine weather and by what the OH likes to call a 'drying breeze'. There was a slight shift in Corps responsibility, with the result that the 33rd Division came up (during the night 24/25 September) to the right of the 1st Australian Division (itself replaced by the 5th on the nights of 22 and 23 September) several hundred yards forward of Black Watch Corner.

The Germans put in their counter stroke just as the relief of the 23rd

View from just north of the site of Carlisle Farm.

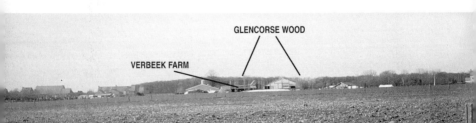

GLENCORSE WOOD

VERBEEK FARM

Division was taking place; when the attack came at 6.00 am (preceded by a forty five minute barrage), the relief of the front line battalions had just been completed, hardly giving the newcomers time to grow accustomed to their surroundings.

1/Middlesex had a particularly difficult time, on the far left of the 33rd Division; to the south and down to the Menin Road the Germans made very little ground. The centre of 1/Middlesex line was just behind Carlisle Farm (ie on the west side of the motorway), with defences that consisted of shell hole posts connected by short lengths of trench. The German defences, in rather better shape, lay to the west of Cameron House and Jut Farm; about midway between the opposing lines was Jerk Farm, also in the possession of the enemy.

The Battalion finally was able to report the relief complete at 4.30 am; on the left the line was held by B Company (C in support), A on the right with D in support. Battalion HQ was on the southern edge of Glencorse Wood. Communications were very difficult because telephone wires were continually being cut by German artillery fire. When the German barrage fell it was intense; that on the 5th Australian Division and 33rd Division fronts involving 27 batteries of field artillery, 17 field howitzer batteries, 15 heavy howitzer batteries and 5 batteries of high velocity long range guns. Gas and heavy shrapnel were also extensively used. There was a thick, heavy morning mist which provided further cover for the German infantry which included an Assault Battalion.

B Company lost three platoons at the centre of its position, though a fourth, on the right, carried on holding its position. The result of this first assault was that there was now a gap between A and B companies; the second wave, attacking at 6.30 am from the direction of Jerk House, managed to work its way through this and get into this part of the Wilhelm Line (also known to the British as Veldhoek Trench) and began to fight their way southward along it. Both companies had lost all their officers, and the two companies made their way back 150 yards or so their support positions.

The support companies were unable to see what was going on because of the mist, and were in any case pinned down by artillery and machine-gun fire. However, once it was clear that the situation in front was critical, Lewis guns were pushed forward into shell holes in the

NONNE BOSSCHEN WOOD

BLACKWATCH CORNER

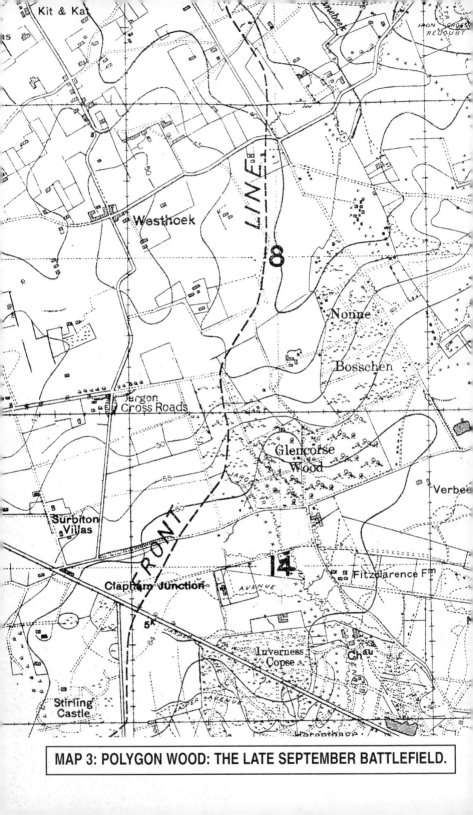

MAP 3: POLYGON WOOD: THE LATE SEPTEMBER BATTLEFIELD.

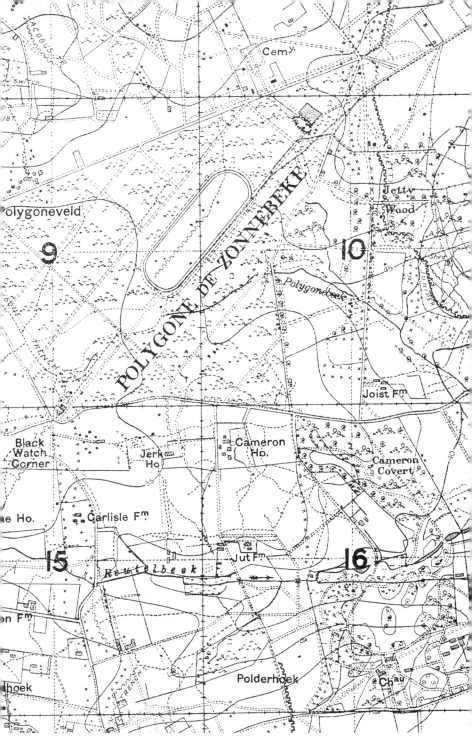

centre and managed to stem the German advance. Battalion HQ now had been able to call upon the assistance of C Company 2/Argyll and Sutherland Highlanders and a platoon was sent forward to ensure that contact was not broken with the Australians. However, before they went forward a runner came back to HQ from No 6 Platoon of B Company, which was still holding its original position on the Australian right, despite frequent frontal assaults and enfilade fire from its right.

> With the situation stabilised, it was decided that an attack should be made to recapture the line J.15.d.4.8 to J.9.d.4.0 (that is, more or less from the Reutelbeek directly north to the south western edge of Polygon Wood) at 2 pm. A mixture of troops from the Argylls and the Middlesex would undertake this attack. This was brought to a halt by a German defensive barrage and heavy machine-gun fire, so that a line had to be dug along the original support position. The platoon of B Company stayed in its position until relieved on the afternoon of 26 September and returned to the rear at Railway Dugouts, whence they had originally come, to the south west of Zillebeke Lake.[8]

The end result was that 98 Brigade was forced back to a line just east of Verbeek Farm, near the Nonne Boschen road, southwards, running a few hundred yards to the west of the road on which was Lone House. On the other hand, they had posts forward of that, but the situation was so confused that no one quite knew how far forward two companies of Argylls and some of 1/Middlesex actually were. In fact they held positions either side of Lone House.

Obviously this made considerable problems for the 5th Australian

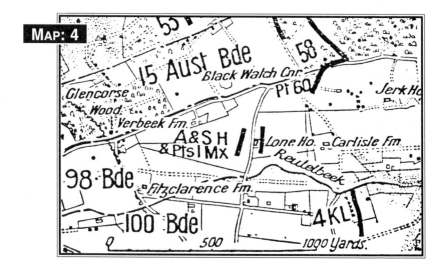

Division – their right flank was highly exposed. It also made it imperative to amend the objectives for the 33rd Division. The Australians brought up battalions from the reserve brigade, the 8th, to replace those which had suffered heavily in hanging on to the right flank, which now had to be manned for some four hundred yards. Indeed 15 Brigade's right flank ran from its front line position to its own support line. The German artillery fire had been so fierce that divisional dumps of ammunition were all destroyed, lines of communications utterly disrupted, and heavy losses had been suffered by troops waiting in the vicinity of Glencorse Wood. New battalions would be required to replace those exhausted in the German counter stroke of the 25th.

To give some idea of how bad the German artillery barrage was, Bean describes the problem facing Major-General Hobbs, commanding the 5th Division, when he tried to get up to see Brigadier-General Elliott (commanding 15 Brigade) at the latter's HQ in Hooge Crater.

> But such was the German barrage on the Menin Road that at 200 yards from Elliott's headquarters he had to turn back. Geysers of earth were springing from the country on either side, raising a dust cloud through which succeeding explosions were faintly visible. Aeroplanes were bombing. The advanced divisional dump of ammunition for the next day's attack had been blown up, and cartridges and bombs were littered on all sides; several motor lorries had been wrecked on the Menin Road, and one was burning fiercely.[9]

In fact there was complete confusion as to what was going on at the front – both amongst the British and the Australians. The action that was causing such dislocation was on the right, along the Reutel road, and then across the knoll that fell away four to five hundred yards to the south, into the valley of the Reutelbeek.

At the end of the battle Elliott was to write a full report and was particularly critical of the role of the 33rd Division in events (as well as of others senior to him). Whilst ably written, it took no account of the problems facing these senior commanders, nor of the particular difficulties facing the right flank division, in this case the 33rd. Bean comments,

> These statements, though he believed them to be true, were definitely untrue and grossly unfair. Birdwood [Anzac Corps Commander], with justice, refused to accept the report and to include it in the official records, but a copy survived.[10]

5/6 Scottish Rifles (Cameronians), 19 Brigade.

Early on the morning of the 25th, Lieutenant-Colonel Spens was ordered to reconnoitre a close support position for the Argylls and Middlesex, battalions which were supposed to be leading the attack on the 26th. In the process of heading up for the line his accompanying officer was killed by a shell near Clapham Junction.

The battalion was then brought up to Clapham Junction via Sanctuary Wood. The approach was none too pleasant for many of those who had gone up the previous night were lying dead all over the place.[11]

Late at night it was determined that the battalion, along with 4/Suffolks, would front the attack for 98 Brigade on the 26th, because of the casualties suffered by the battalions earmarked for that task.

The ground in front was new to us, and guides from the front battalions were asked for. The night was dark and the shelling worse than ever. Battalion headquarters had been established near some friendly looking tanks which appeared to be on fairly firm ground at L Farm, formerly an old road running north and south past Fitzclarence Farm. The surrounding ground was a mass of shell holes filled with stinking water and mud and if you fell in you were lost. It was every man for himself, and no one who passed through that night is ever likely to forget its tragedies. It seemed safest to keep to the road, so out the party stretched in India file in the dark with the guide and the Colonel in front. For an hour the party followed the lead. Fires were observed burning fiercely, and as the party drew near it found itself back at the place from which it had started. The tanks were now a blazing mass of twisted iron. What had gone wrong with the guide? He was obviously lost and had been walking in a circle. The Colonel was heard expressing his opinion, and eventually the guide took fright and disappeared.

Pillboxes at Polygon Wood, and the butte, seen from the front line of the 7th Brigade, 21st September, 1917.

The situation was chaotic, with companies losing touch with each other. The Battalion was supposed to be attacking at 5.50 am, and indeed by that stage was supposed to have relieved the Argylls and Middlesex, but no-one was quite sure where anyone was, and in the meantime there were casualties. Even when daylight came things were not much better – a combination of mist, smoke and dust from the shelling obscured everything.

In the end, all that the battalion managed to effect was to join up with the Argylls and the Middlesex in their line, and where possible relieved them from their positions forward of Black Watch Corner. The Battalion then proceeded to dig in to this position. On the brigade's right 100 Brigade was to hold fast – which they did, having successfully beaten off the German attack along the valley of the Reutelbeek, whilst ground lost on the 25th adjacent to the Menin Road was recaptured.

One of the big problems lay in the number of low flying German aircraft, a considerable number of which were brought down by machine-gun and rifle fire; and the increasing frequency of German bombing raids behind the lines – several histories record this, and the fact that this bombing became a normal event for the rest of the war.

The 33rd Division was required to take its objectives on the 27th, which was achieved with the assistance of the Australians and by the men of the Scottish Rifles and 2/RWF (Royal Welsh Fusiliers). The main centre of German resistance was around Jut farm, with its nearby pill boxes, so that by the early evening 98 Brigade was sitting on its revised objective for the attack. Later that night it was relieved by elements of the 23rd Division.

What is certain that the activities of the 33rd Division were not of much assistance to the Australians on their left, who had Polygon Wood as their objective; their boundary with the 33rd Division was the road running along the southern edge of the wood, and the German presence on their flank was to cause considerable difficulties for the 5th Division.

The 5th (Australian) Division captures Polygon Wood.
Preparations

The 5th Division had been effectively out of the fighting for five months, and in a rest area for four of these – though 'rest' in the Great War was never what we associate with the term. Indeed, this battle at Polygon Wood was to be the Division's first set-piece battle since its unfortunate first encounter with the Western Front at Fromelles, in July

1916; though it had been present at parts of the Bullecourt fighting.

The wood which formed the bulk of the Division's objective was called Polygon, partly because there were roughly five sides (though not all equal, and somewhat ragged at that, with an extension to the wood coming off the east side), partly because it was, in earlier years, an artillery school. The 5th Division history states that the mound (on which now stands the divisional memorial) was a stop butte for the artillery that used to train there. This seems a little implausible; it almost certainly was a rifle butte at some stage in its history. The racecourse was originally used to train horses and gunners in their work with limbers, but had also been used to train for equestrian events. Indeed some officers were rebuked for jumping the fences during the early stages of First Ypres; Lyn Macdonald's *1914* saying that the Belgian team for Olympia did its training here.

Although most of the trees had been shot away, there still existed a thick undergrowth about three feet in height, through which the remains of old trench systems and wire entanglements ran in all directions, greatly complicating the passage of troops. A little stream, the Polgonbeek, rising near the south extremity of the riding track, passed in a south east direction across the right half of the divisional objective area and later joined the Reutelbeek, another tiny stream, which flowed east out of the right hand area of 98 Brigade. On the 98 Brigade front there were, about two hundred and fifty yards to the right of the 5th Divisional boundary, a sequence of three strong positions known as Jerk House, Cameron House and Cameron Covert (or Copse).[12]

Troops engaged in the battle in the part of the salient were billeted to the south west, around Dickebusch and Ouderdom (where there was a very large railhead). The approach to the front either went through Ypres itself, past the Menin Gate (actually only a gap in the ramparts), along the Menin Road, the via sacra of the British army, past Birr Crossroads and Hooge, to the tracks leading off from Clapham Junction. The alternative was a cross-country route, which at least had the merit of avoiding the constant shelling of the shattered town and the scamper across Hell Fire corner. This meant heading towards Ypres until Café Belge and turning right to Kruistraathoek, then turning left to Shrapnel Corner.

All this was the area of long range guns and giant howitzers, of captive balloons, of artillery wagon lines and of reserve infantry units.

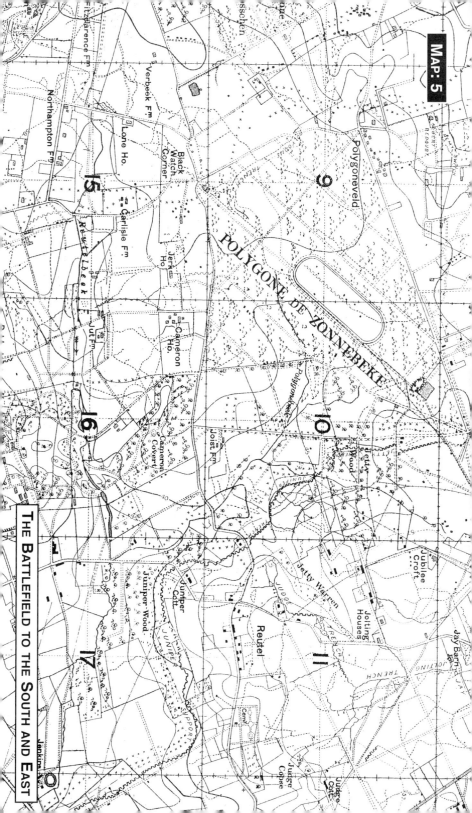

Fitzclarence F^m

Northampton F^m

Verbeek F^m

Lone Ho.

Black Watch Corner

15

Carlisle F^m

Jerk Ho.

Reutelbeek

Jut F^m

Cameron Ho.

16

Cameron Covert

Joist F^m

17

Juniper Wood

Juniper Cott

Cameron Covert

40

Polygoneveld

9

POLYGONE DE ZONNEBEKE

Polygonebeek

REDOUBT

10

Jetty Wood

Jetty Warren

JUDGE TRENCH

Reutel

11

Jolting Houses

Jubilee Croft

Jay Barn

JOLTING

Judge Copse

Judge Cott

Camp

SUPPORT

Jenkins

The 7th Field Artillery Brigade moving forward to Bellewaarde Ridge on September 21st in preparation for the next stage of the battle on the Australian sector, Polygon Wood. Each of the grey pack-horses is carrying eight shells and charges for the field-guns.

At Shrapnel Corner 'steel helmets were adjusted'; then there was a right turn along Warrington Road, a long corduroy track, which lead past numerous batteries along the north of Zillebeke Lake (in the dugouts of the railway embankments to the south of the lake was the home of numerous battalions in support to those in the line at Polygon Wood). The track then became a mule path past Halfway House, Leinster Farm and on to Zouave Wood, to the south of Hooge. The track went on through Zouave Wood, crossed the Menin Road near Clapham Junction and from there on to Glencorse Wood, Nonne Boschen and finally to the front line. For the last three and a half miles, more or less from Shrapnel Corner onwards, the route was under continual shell fire, with especial attention given to Glencorse Wood and Hooge.

The attack was to have two phases; this was to allow for reorganisation and for assault battalions for the second objective to pass through. Just as the Germans had adapted their defensive strategy since the Somme, using their counter-attack divisions, so the British countered by adopting a policy of attack with positions then held in depth – which proved to be, generally, extremely effective. The attack on Polygon Wood was to have two objectives. The first was to move the front forward some 750 yards to the Red Line, which was effectively the eastern edge of the modern Polygon Wood, minus a small section in the north east corner. The second phase of the attack would move the line a further 350 yards to the Blue Line, which would include the capture of Joist Farm, Jetty Wood, Jetty Trench and Juniper Trench. 15 Brigade would attack on the right, 14 Brigade on the left and 8 Brigade would be in reserve, with each of the assaulting brigades responsible for a front of approximately 550 yards.

The assault would be carried out by one battalion, attacking on a two company front following closely the artillery barrage, which would move forward (or creep), from a point 150 yards ahead of the start line, at the rate of six minutes for every hundred yards. This was designed to give the attackers protection from the scattered German pill boxes, preventing the garrisons from debouching and bringing their machine-guns to bear until the assaulting infantry was almost upon them. Once at the Red Line the barrage would halt for an hour whilst each brigade brought forward two other battalions, which would then move forward on a one company front to take the Blue Line. The

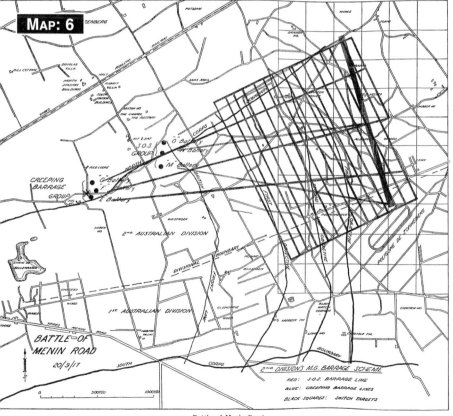

Battle of Menin Road.

second stage of the advance would be slower, so the creeping barrage moved forward at the rate of eight minutes per hundred yards. On arrival at the final objective an outpost line would be thrown forward and strong posts established three hundred yards behind them – in short it was an attack in depth to be followed by a defence in depth.

The reserve battalion of 8 Brigade was held at Halfway House, which was also the location of the Brigade Headquarters. The rest of the reserve brigade's battalions were at Chateau Segard (which was also the Divisional Battle Headquarters), a mile and a half east of Dickebusch. The headquarters of the two forward brigades were situated in deep dugouts in Hooge Crater.

In addition to the massive artillery cover, a large number of Vickers guns were also to provide a barrage of their own, as well as providing support for the newly established lines.

Every division had 64 of these guns; for the battle the Australians received further guns and teams to man them. A creeping barrage was to be provided by three groups (each group had eight guns) positioned in Glencorse Wood; four groups were to provide an SOS barrage before the front line (wherever it might be established) and were positioned some four hundred yards behind the Assembly Line. Each brigade was given eight mobile guns, to be used wherever they might best assist the process of consolidation; whilst a reserve of sixteen guns was held to be used as necessary. Pioneers and engineers were to mark out a track to the assembly point on each brigade front (pickets were to be panted white at the top); signposts put up; drainage of tracks was to be carried out; concertina wire was to be put out in front of the strong post line as soon as possible, with further wiring of the line behind; and two strong points were to be constructed behind the Red Line on each brigade front. In addition bridging material was required for crossing the Polygonbeek.

Communication was to be covered by a mixture of every technology available, ranging from pigeons (three pairs to each battalion headquarters), power buzzers, buried cable, visual stations, a forward wireless set, runner routes marked out by flags and a system of communicating with the contact aircraft of the RFC, itself distinguished from others by the black streamer on the rear edge of its left wing.

Elaborate arrangements were made for the immediate collection of information from the battlefield. An Intelligence Policeman who could speak German was attached to each infantry battalion to get information of vital local tactical importance as soon as possible after the capture of any prisoners. Each Intelligence Policeman was given four men to assist him in searching the battlefield for important documents. Prisoners of war were to be hurried back to Captain Robinson, the Divisional Intelligence Officer at Hooge Crater, where any information likely to be urgently required in the battle was extracted from them... Officers, NCOs and men were to be kept separated as far as practicable.

Numerous other factors were also carefully planned for – water supply (cans at Hooge); pack horse transport and ration supply; ordnance dumps; traffic control posts; RE dumps; and burial parties. A nucleus of men - either the battalion commander or his second in command, all officers over a maximum number of twenty allowed in each battalion and at least 108 men of all ranks – was kept back at Caestre, some miles to the west, over the French border.

And the most vital support of all to the operation was the scale of the artillery provided – approximately one heavy gun for every ten yards of front, to be accompanied by the 18-pounders and 4.5 inch howitzers of the field artillery brigades.

To ensure that as many people as possible had a clear idea of the countryside over which they would be operating, men went to look at the vast scale model, several thousand square yards in extent, which had been constructed at Busseboom, a village between Ouderdom and Poperinghe. The model showed every topographical feature of any significance – wood, stream, ridge, road – and markers showed the progress of the battle thus far.

The events of 25 September had severely shaken the plans of 15 Brigade. Once it was clear what the German intentions were, Major-General Hobbs at 8 pm ordered up two battalions of 8 Brigade to come up and replace those who had been tied into the fighting on the right flank of the division's position. This gave them over nine hours to get from Chateau Segard to the assembly positions, a distance of six miles as the crow flies, but in fact barely adequate to get them up to the line. The shelling had died down, but the men had heavy burdens, and the whole area was bustling with military activity. The men took up their position along their taped positions in silence, the Germans quite unaware as to what was going on, whilst the three attacking battalions set up their headquarters at Black Watch Corner. Indeed Crown Prince Rupprecht had noted after his counter stroke of 25 September, which he thought had succeeded, 'the next enemy major attack will presumably not follow until after a few day' and felt confident enough to leave for Munich to deal with urgent personal matters.

The Attack

It is one of the realities of battles that an account of an entirely successful attack takes far less space than one in which there are difficulties before the objective is achieved. For this reason the battle is described from right to left, instead of the customary left to right, thereby covering the battle from the least troublesome to the most, at least so far as Polygon Wood is concerned.

Bean reports the start of the battle.

> *The barrage which descended at 5.50 am on September 26th, just as the Polygon plateau became visible, was the most perfect that ever protected Australian troops. It seemed to break out, as almost every report emphasises, with a single crash. The ground was dry, and the shell bursts raised a wall of dust and smoke which appeared almost to be solid. So dense was the cloud that individual bursts, except the white bursts of shrapnel above its near edge, could not be distinguished. Roaring, deafening, it rolled ahead of the troops 'like a Gippsland bush fire'. Its very density carried one disadvantage; in such a fog it was difficult to discern where the actual line of shell bursts lay, except by running into them. Direction had to be kept by officers with compass in hand.*

The attack involved two Australian (4th and 5th) and five British divisions; three of the latter were on the Australian left and two,

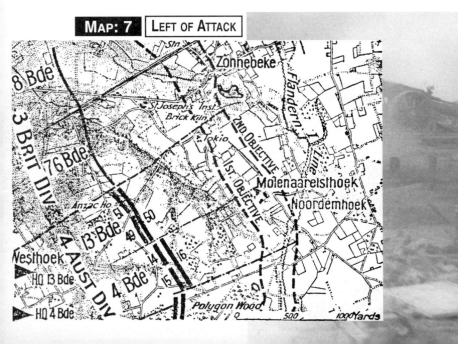

MAP: 7 | LEFT OF ATTACK

including the 33rd, on the right.

The 4th Australian Division faced the problem that the Broodseinde Ridge, well beyond the objective, overlooked its advance. The advantage was that it made it very difficult indeed for the German counter-attack unless by night (by which time the Australians would have been well dug in). If they attacked in daylight as soon as they moved over the crest and down the exposed slope they would be vulnerable not only to the withering defensive fire of the infantry, but would be subjected to a mighty defensive artillery barrage.

In this case the interest lies in 4 Brigade, whose right boundary was a hundred yards or so to the north of the northern road around Polygon Wood. On this right flank the first objective lay just beyond what is now Polygon Wood cemetery. The only significant problems faced in this attack lay with a number of German pillboxes and a tendency for men to run into the barrage, especially after reaching the first objective. Natural exuberance led some to forget that there was a significant pause at this point, to allow fresh men to come forward to take on the second objective.

The Red Line, the first objective, was the road running north north west from the north eastern tip of the wood, some 750 yards beyond the British line. The second objective, the Blue Line, lay three hundred metres or so further east, following the Zonnebeke road to Die Veldhoek, where it turned southwards, running in front of Jetty Wood.

The great weight of British artillery proved decisive in the battles of late September and early October.

This involved, on the left flank of the 5th Division, breaking the German Flanders I Line. 16 Battalion was to take the first objective, whilst 14 Battalion on the left and 15 Battalion on the right were to go through and take the second.

The 14th Battalion AIF was often known to members of the Australian Imperial Force as 'Jacka's Mob'.

> *The ground over which the attack took place was in a frightful state, in places knee-deep in mud. There were shell holes every few yards, most of them filled with water. These conditions made the going very arduous, particularly as very little sleep had been obtained by the combatants on the previous night. Excitement and the prospect of victory, however, supplied the necessary tonic to face the difficulties ahead.*[13]

The 16th had faced difficulties from pill boxes on its left flank, but with the aid of men from the 14th, led by Captain Jacka, these were overcome, and in due course the second phase of the attack went ahead.

> *As the advance progressed the opposition stiffened, and the machine-gun fire of the enemy became greater, causing a fair number of casualties. Several enemy machine-guns and their crews were captured, one machine-gunner captured being chained to his gun. Few of the enemy outside the pill boxes waited for our barrage, though some did, and occasionally a German would fly up skyward as one of our shells lobbed in a hole beside him. The majority, however, either bolted through the barrage, or retired before its advent, forming excellent targets for our men, of which they took full advantage.*

'The ground over which the attack took place was in a frightful state, in places knee-deep in mud.'

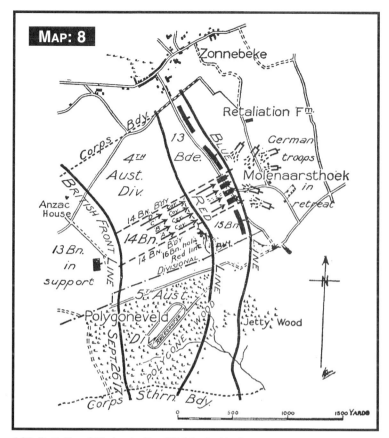

14th Battalion (4th Australian Division) attack.

The problem of coming too close to the barrage led some of the leading men to turn back, to avoid being killed by 'friendly fire'; seeing this, others behind them also turned. The situation was resolved by the prompt action of Captain Jacka, who ran forward, disregarding the barrage and rallied the men into following him. The second objective was reached by 8 am, but the battalion was pushed forward by the company commanders a further forty or fifty yards beyond it; this was a sensible precaution, as when the German barrage fell for their own attacks, it fell on the road. Casualties would have been very high if the men had dug in there, as was originally intended.

The battalion historian is somewhat critical of the decision to stop there, rather than pressing on and taking the Broodseinde Ridge, which the Germans were streaming over in some disorder; in due course they returned, and its eventual capture was to be most expensive in men. However, he does not take into account what was happening on the flanks, nor of the capacity of the Germans to recover and counter-

47

attack, nor, indeed, of the ability of the artillery to either support such an action or, more importantly, to defend the position with adequate defensive fire afterwards.

On arrival at the second objective, Captain Harold Wanliss, commanding A Company, was killed by a German machine-gun which he was trying to locate.

Bean comments

> *This was a grievous loss. By his friends, including General Monash, Colonels Peck and Durrant, Chaplain Rolland and men of all ranks, Harold Wanliss had been recognised as a young man possibly destined, had he lived, to lead Australia. Peck, formerly his battalion commander, wrote: 'Many brave men, many good men I have met...but he was the king of them all'. He added that he 'cursed the day' that had deprived him of the chance of preserving Wanliss's life. ...He had studied agriculture..and had taken up land just before the war. His periods of furlough he had devoted to study of industry new to Australia, which he would endeavour to introduce there after the war.*

He had won the DSO, gazetted in July 1916, for his bravery in leading an attacking party during a raid in the Bois Grenier sector, the first launched by the 4th Australian Division since its arrival in France.

> *He forced the wire which was uncut, entered the trench, inflicted heavy loss on the enemy and supervised the withdrawal. While forcing the wire he was wounded in the face, later he was wounded by a bullet in the neck, and finally when withdrawing he was again wounded and had to be carried in.* [London Gazette, 27 July 1916]

According to one authority, he was the first Australian subaltern to be awarded the DSO in the Great War. His father was the author of the Battalion history. Captain Albert Jacka VC MC and Bar commented that, he was a hero and a man. He has no known grave and is commemorated on the Menin Gate. All the Australian and Canadian missing in Belgium are listed here; those in France are on the memorials at Villers-Brettonneux or Vimy Ridge respectively.

The 14th Battalion held the line against several attempted German counter-attacks before they were relieved on the 28th; and of course had to put up with incessant artillery fire. The battalion historian says of Jacka,

> *The present engagement was an outstanding triumph for Captain Jacka. His personal achievements in previous battles*

had been the admiration of his countrymen, but at Polygon Wood, when the opportunity came, he displayed in addition a power of leadership, a grasp of tactics and a military intuition that many had not given him credit for. It is impossible to over-estimate the value of his services during those three days in the line. He carried the left wing of the battalion forward with a magnificent dash to the second objective, and there took practical control of the unit, and was thereafter the guiding spirit of the storm of battle. His reckless valour, his excellent judgement, his skilful tactics, his prompt anticipation of the enemy's movements, and the force and vigour of his battle strokes gained the admiration of all ranks, and inspired everyone with the greatest confidence. Throughout the whole engagement he was a ubiquitous and fearless figure, the very incarnation of a great fighting soldier and a born leader of men. No more fearless or gallant soldier took part in the Great War.

Captain Albert Jacka

The author goes on to congratulate the Intelligence Officer for his hard work, noting somewhat cuttingly, 'he appears to have been the only officer from Battalion Headquarters at the front line during the engagement'.

The Regimental Aid Post was located in a pill box alongside Battalion Headquarters during the engagement, but owing to the non-receipt by the company commanders of a message sent by the RMO [Regimental Medical Officer] as to its locality, few of the 14th wounded were passed to it, most of them going to, and being treated at, the RAP of the 15th Battalion. Owing to the heavy and continuous enemy barrages the duties of the stretcher-bearers proved exceptionally dangerous, with consequent heavy casualties. They, however, worked unceasingly, with their usual gallantry. Thirty-two

49

stretcher-bearers took part in the engagement, and at its conclusion only seven of them were fit for duty, and the whole of the eight stretchers, and most of the equipment, had been destroyed by enemy action.

The Battalion went into action some five hundred strong; most of the casualties took place on the 26th. In total there were 170, of which 3 officers and 37 other ranks were killed, the rest wounded with seven other ranks missing.

The 5th Australian Division.

The right attacking brigade was the 14th, under the command of Brigadier-General Hobkirk. They, too, had a relatively painless time, though this is only in the context of success and a number of casualties that were made tolerable by the extent of that success.

53 Battalion spent the day before the attack in Nonne Boschen Wood, a place detested because it was a favourite target for German artillery trying to disrupt the offensive plans and the supply of supplies ad men to the front line.

There it caught in full the tremendous bombardments of September 25th and by evening had lost 150 men. Its ration party was gassed; many had to eat their emergency rations, and fill their waterbottles from shell holes. Yet this hard grained force was in keen spirit when at midnight it moved to its tapes.

To avoid the German barrage, Hobkirk had his three assaulting battalions (all twelve waves of them) closed up in a stretch of ground only sixty yards wide; 53rd at the front, 55th on the left and 56th on the right. Thus when a German barrage came down at 4 am, the standard precautionary blast of their artillery, it missed them. On the

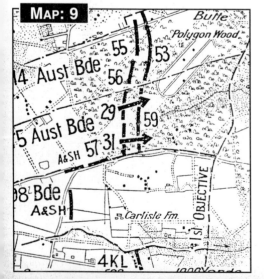

other hand a single shell had caused havoc to the 56th Battalion on its way up. In Chateau Wood, to the north east of Hooge, it knocked out the adjutant, the signalling officer and most of his men, as well as the medical officer. This latter was Captain GS Elliott MC, the brother of Brigadier-General Elliott, commanding 15 Brigade. He is buried in Huts Cemetery, Dickebusch.

The Butte, Polygon Wood. This mound, which stood on the far side of Polygon Wood, was taken by the 5th Australian Division.

When the time for the attack came, all went smoothly. The 55th reported that Captain Cotterell led its advance at a stroll, 'cigarette in mouth, map in hand, behind him the thick line of worm columns each led by an NCO'. This officer was killed towards the end of the war.

All pillboxes were immediately outflanked. From some came whimpering boys, holding out hands full of souvenirs. After an unhindered advance of 500 yards, the silhouette of the Butte showed up in the fog. A few figures of German machine-gunners were seen upon it , but they quickly ran off, and the 53rd swarmed over it and bombed the entrances of dugouts on the farther side. On the left, from the cemetery and pillboxes beside it, once a regimental headquarters, machine-guns fired. The place was forthwith seized. In the Butte dugouts 60 Germans, largely medical personnel, surrendered after firing a few shots up the stairs.

Two of these pillboxes captured by the 56th Battalion may be seen in the wood today; one was named Scott Post after the CO of the 56th.[14]

The Red Line for the brigade included the Butte and the cemetery

Scott Post today, the largest remnant of the wood's defences.

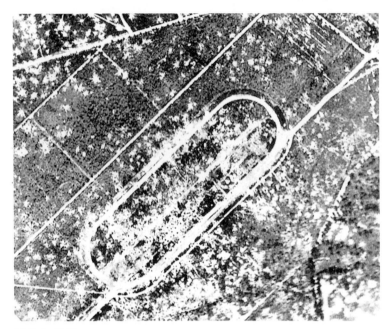

22 July 1917.

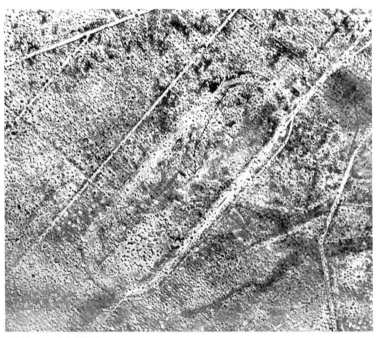

14 September 1917.

to its left. This cemetery was beyond the present British one, and indeed remained in existence as a German military cemetery until the clearance of nearly all the German military cemeteries in the area to Langemark or Menen after the Second World War.

The Blue Line included a considerable length of the Flanders I (or *Flandern*) Line, some thousand yards of it. It was only recognisable by 'shreds of the entanglements', so devastating had been the artillery barrage; the pillboxes that remained were easily taken. Trouble came from the right, in the 15 Brigade area, whose 29th Battalion had not yet come up. Machine-gun and rifle fire came from the vicinity of the German headquarters by the Polygonbeek which, at the time, was short of the barrage. This was suppressed in due course, and two bunkers beyond the objective also had to be tackled, which resulted in the capture of 45 Germans (see below for further details about this post, commanded by Captain Fischer). However, these had to be given up as the defending barrage fire fell west of them. German attempts at counter-attacks were easily broken up; once more, the topography was an advantage to the defenders due to the exposed approach that the Germans had to make in order to counter-attack.

Sergeant JJ Dwyer of the 4th Machine Gun Company won a VC for the resolute manner with which he dealt with a machine-gun on the right flank of the 4th Division attack, in the vicinity of Molenaarelsthoek.

Sergeant Dwyer, in charge of a Vickers machine-gun, went forward with the first wave of the brigade. On reaching the final objective, this non-commissioned officer rushed his gun forward in advance of the captured position, in order to obtain a commanding spot. Whilst advancing he noticed an enemy machine-gun firing on the troops on our right flank and causing casualties. Unhesitatingly he rushed his gun forward within thirty yards of the enemy gun and fired point-bank at it, putting it out of action and killing the gun crew. He then seized the gun, and totally ignoring the snipers from the rear of the enemy position, carried it back across the shell swept ground to our front line, and established both it and his Vickers gun on the right flank of our brigade. Sergeant Dwyer commanded these guns with great coolness, and when the enemy counter-attacked our positions he rendered great assistance in repulsing them. On the following day, when the position was heavily shelled, this non-commissioned officer took up successive positions. On one occasion his Vickers gun was blown up by shell fire, but he

It was near this junction, somewhere to the left, that Sergeant Dwyer won his VC. Molenaarelsthoek is where the modern houses are.

Sergeant Dwyer,

conducted his gun team back to Headquarters through the barrage, secured one of the reserve guns, and rushed it back to our position in the shortest possible time. During the whole of the attack his contempt of danger, cheerfulness and courage raised the spirits of all who were in his sector of the line.

Dwyer was commissioned in the field (in May 1918). He survived the war, became active in local politics and eventually became Deputy Premier of Tasmania. He died in 1962, aged 64.

Perhaps the most significant casualty was Lieutenant-Colonel Croshaw, commanding officer of the 53rd, who died of his wounds and is buried in Bedford House Cemetery (Enclosure Number 2). He was described by Bean as 'one of the noblest officers in the AIF'.

Before the advance he said to his officers: 'Gentlemen, your men before yourselves. Look to your flanks. God bless you lads, till we meet again'. He moved in the centre of the battalion, but few saw him fall. His adjutant was hit at the same time. Croshaw had joined the AIF in Egypt, and was devoted to his men. The chaplain of his unit describes him as 'the bravest soldier, the most God-fearing christian, and the most perfect gentleman I have ever known.'[15]

The 5th Australian Division: the right of the attack.

As has been shown from the events of 25 September, things were far from straightforward on the front of 15 Brigade and the 33rd Division – and indeed of the 39th Division on the south side of the Menin Road.

The operation planned by Brigadier-General Elliott had been upset by the need to commit various of his battalions to assist in the restoration of his right flank. This meant that he was given two

battalions from 8 Brigade to make up his assaulting force for the second objective. The decision to commit these had to be left as late as possible because of the fluid situation on the right flank and a disinclination to commit half the reserve brigade's force before the battle had even begun. There also came into play the problem of different tactical instructions in the different brigades. The men of 8 Brigade were instructed to keep close to the barrage under all circumstances. Thus, when the 59th set off, with its thin screen in front, the remainder following at suitable distances, they suddenly found themselves intermingled with the men of the 29th and 31st battalions who were eagerly seeking to come up to the protective barrage wall of iron and fire. Elliott blamed himself for this situation subsequently, for not making his views clear to the new battalion commanders about distances. In the circumstances his error is understandable – a hard and unexpected fight before his battle, the proceeding of which was in the balance, and who had just lost a brother – some things were bound to be forgotten in the heat of the moment. In addition, the 31st battalion only got into position some ten minutes before zero. Perhaps most ominously, it was becoming quite clear that the right flank was going to be the source of considerable problems, as it was highly unlikely that the 33rd Division would be in any state to begin an advance at zero, with the left attacking battalion trying to find its way out of Inverness Copse only two hours before the attack was due to begin.

The advance of 15 Brigade became chaotic, with a mass of three battalions heading ever onwards, and even elements of the 59th being swept on towards the second objective.

The area traversed, previously empty, had since yesterday been thickly held by the Germans, especially machine-gunners, protecting the right flank of the 229th RIR [Reserve Infantry Regiment, which had bitten into the 33rd Division line the preceding day]. *Lieutenant Gullett, intelligence officer of the 29th, who went with his battalion, noted 'about 18 (German)*

German bunker on the southern edge of Polygon Wood, captured by the 29 Battalion.

machine-guns' firing here or there through the barrage. As the troops sighted one or another close ahead through the fog, the line might for a moment ripple, but the swing suddenly towards the gun from all sides. Usually the Germans threw up their hands in the vain hope of mercy, but Gullett saw one German who kept his thumbs on the button until a bayonet drove into his chest. Some of the enemy showed fight at two pillboxes in the south-west corner of the wood [these bunkers still exist], *and at another on the so-called racecourse, and machine-guns fired from the Butte, outside the Brigade's area.*

This phase of the battle was proving to be expensive. Further confusion was caused when many in the 59th thought that part of the racecourse, recognisable by its remnants of light railway, was the first objective, when in fact this was 150 yards short.

The real problem came from the right, however. The exposed flank meant that the men of the 31st came under fire from the right and, indeed, from the rear. Men of the 57th and 60th battalions guarded

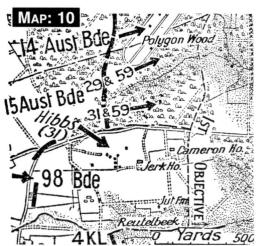

56

the flank, but it was not enough to fend off harassing fire. The problem also meant that men deviated from their course and veered towards the sources of the hostile fire, so that the right boundary was crossed in an attempt to eliminate them. This procedure also meant that the confusion with the 31st Battalion was made worse, as the actions to remove these pillboxes slowed down the rate of advance of the 59th.

An example of this tendency to seep over the boundary was the capture by men of the 31st of a German pillbox and its four machine-guns some 200 yards outside the divisional boundary. The accepted method for dealing with the pillboxes was as follows:

> A couple of Lewis guns would open on the defenders and rifle bombers would drop their volleys of grenades all around them. Under cover of this fire a couple of parties would work round the flank of the obstruction and in a few moments further resistance was impossible.

The advance to the Red Line was more or less to time, with a pause of an hour under the protection of an artillery barrage which allowed for reorganisation before the advance was to continue again at 7.30 am for the final 350 yards - which would bring Joist Farm and Juniper Trench into Australian hands. As the advance to the Red Line continued, so the backbone of the German resistance crumbled.

> For a time the scene was exciting, Germans running in all directions like so many bewildered rabbits, and resolute Australians rounding them up and shooting down those who refused to surrender. Enemy aeroplanes, too, added to the commotion, and one, firing from about thirty feet at a party of men consolidating, was brought down so suddenly by their rifle fire that the men could scarcely dodge the falling machine. The 15th LTMB [Light Trench Mortar Battery] sub-sections were doing excellent work, silencing strong points and, later on, helping to sustain the right flank.

The right hand company, commanded by Captain Hibbs, of the 31st had swung around to the south to deal with a group of pillboxes to the west of Jerk House. These had been too close to the British line to be covered by the barrage, and put up a stubborn defence.

One of the principal motivators in this onslaught on the Germans was Private Paddy Bugden, a Lewis gunner. His VC citation (gazetted on 26 November 1917) is for his bravery and devotion to duty

> when on two occasions our advance was temporarily held up by strongly defended pill-boxes. Private Bugden, in the face of devastating fire from machine-guns, led small parties to attack

these strong points and, successfully silencing the machine-guns with bombs, captured the garrison at the point of the bayonet. On another occasion, when a corporal, who had become detached from his company, had been captured and was being taken to the rear by the enemy, Private Bugden single-handed rushed to the rescue of his comrade, shot one enemy and bayoneted the remaining two, thus releasing the corporal. On five occasions he rescued wounded men under intense shell and machine-gun fire, showing an utter contempt and disregard for danger. Always foremost in volunteering for any dangerous mission, it was in the execution of one of these missions that this gallant soldier was killed.

He was killed on 28 September and was buried on the edge of Glencorse Wood in a fenced off grave with an ornate wooden cross placed over it. He is now buried at Hooge Crater Cemetery.

Eventually the men ran out of steam, their energy sapped by the need to take one pillbox after another; and they were eventually driven to ground a hundred yards or so from Jerk House. Their right flank was completely in the air, and the position was such that it was difficult to give supporting fire from the 33rd Division's right or from the Australian lines.

Originally buried in Glencorse Wood, he is now in Hooge Crater Cemetery.

It was evident that they could not stay there, and the only alternative was to capture Jerk House. Officer after officer was killed: Lieutenant Brodie; Lieutenant Rose and Captain Hibbs. The nature of the fighting in this area over the next hours and days is perhaps best indicated by the fact that none of their bodies were recovered, and their names are to be found on the Menin Gate.

The 31st now had a thin line which stretched some two hundred yards into the 33rd Division area, but it was reinforced by trench mortars and members of the LTMB, commanded by Lieutenant Hill.

The situation was not good; the men were pinned down in front of Jerk House

> where numerous German machine-guns were most vigorously handled. Germans were assembling at the post there, and Lieutenant Hill, while keeping watch on them, had his eye shot out. He still tried to direct, but most of his men were hit. The enemy made a swift counter thrust and captured him with an officer of the 29th [which shows just how confused 15 Brigade's attack had become!] and about twenty men, fourteen of whom were wounded.

It was at this stage that Bugden rescued the corporal, whose name was Alf Thompson.

> I was out in a shell hole in front and did not get the order to retire so I did not know that I was left on my own. When Fritz counter-attacked us I got two of them with my rifle but I had to duck down in the shell-hole owing to a machine-gun firing on me. Just then three Fritzes tumbled into the shell-hole on top of me giving me no chance to put up a scrap. They immediately disarmed me and the youngest Fritz, who was about eighteen

A captured German pillbox. Most of the pillboxes in the Salient were far less complex than this one.

years of age, put his revolver at my head and was going to shoot. The eldest Fritz of the three started gibbering away in German and eventually made the young Fritz take his revolver away from my head (much to my relief!). A moment or so after ... the Fritz who had just saved me from being shot made a jump into the next shell-hole and got shot through the stomach. I looked up to see what was happening and saw a private named Paddy Bugden charging up with a few men to my rescue. The other two Fritzes made to get away and Bugden quickly finished them off and I was then able to get back to our lines safely. The whole ... episode took place under very heavy shell, rifle and machine-gun fire, so you can understand the debt I owe to Paddy Bugden for his bravery in rescuing me. [17]

Jerk House was a stubborn centre of resistance, comparable to the line of pill boxes commanded by Captain Fischer in the Flanders I line by the Polygonbeek (see below). Major Hethey commanded the Germans, themselves from a variety of units, in the area to the south of Polygon Wood down towards the Reutelbeek.

Major Hethey's counter-attack was made with half of II Battalion of 229 RIR, and the Germans claim thirty prisoners. But the fight was as costly in German as in Australian officers. Major Hethey was shot

Aerial view of the eastern part of Polygon Wood and the ground to the south.

through the head directing the defence. Lieutenant Glaubitz, who succeeded him, and Lieutenant Weigel were shot in the same way about 7 o'clock, and Lieutenant Stölting (of the machine-gun company) through the heart at 7.30.

The 31st, now on the Red Line, suffered heavy fire from Cameron House; Major Tracey decided that the only sensible thing to do was to swing his right flank back and formed a line facing south. He had to give these orders by signal – the uproar made verbal communications impossible – which led to some misunderstanding and a more general withdrawal, which was however soon rectified.

There was now a rather longer halt than anticipated on the Red Line. Lieutenant-Colonel Toll, commanding the 31st Battalion, was understandably anxious about proceeding further with his right flank still in the air and his men in a hopeless muddle with the 59th. In any case, he had been assured that the 33rd Division would come up in due course, and he was willing to give them the time so to do. In any case, his battalion had been engaged more than had been anticipated, and had suffered a considerable number of casualties. Taking his cue from Toll, Lieutenant-Colonel Purser of the 29th also delayed (this decision had a slight knock-on effect on 14 Brigade), but at noon they determined to press on to the Blue Line. Purser's decision was

Brigadier-General H. E. Elliott.

questionable, and led to confusion – one officer took his company on regardless, following the barrage; whilst many of Toll's men did not receive the order and began to advance only to be called back.

> *Toll's message to Elliott, informing him of the decision to hold up the attack, brought from that vigorous commander a characteristic order to go on or be superseded. Toll endeavoured to carry out Elliott's wish but, his troops being scattered and inextricably intermingled with the 59th, swift compliance was impossible. It was typical of Elliott that thenceforward he dealt chiefly directly with Lieutenant-Colonel Marshall* [commanding the 60th Battalion], *thus placing Toll, whom he had not actually superseded, in a difficult position.*[18]

The 29th made rapid progress, and within the hour was on its objective; thus reports the history,

61

APPROXIMATE SITE OF CAPT FISCHER

POLYGONBEEK

AUSTRALIAN ADVANCE

Looking along the eastern edge from the south of Polygon Wood. The German main position was centre right.

and Purser's own report. In fact the 29th was on its second objective by 9.45 am. What happened was that the 59th were discovered, by Captain Neale, to be digging in on the racecourse, about 200 yards short of the Red Line, which was situated just beyond the bed of the Polygonbeek on a small crest. There were some men of 8 Brigade digging there, but most were making their way back towards the racecourse position.

At this stage the men forward, they came under fire from an old German battery position on the objective line, the eastern edge of Polygon Wood. The defenders fell back, however, to a line of pillboxes where the Polygonbeek crossed the Blue Line. This advance took place at approximately 7.30 am, ie when the second phase of the attack should have commenced.

At this stage the Germans in the pillboxes launched a counter-attack, which aimed to take 14 Brigade's right in the flank and rear as they began their advance to the Second Objective. Captain Fischer, the battalion commander of the right or the 229th RIR, personally led this resolute local German action. This position should have been attacked, according to the programme, by the 29th at the same time as 14 Brigade set off. Fischer was wounded in the attack, and at a key moment Neale's line arrived, sending the Germans back to their pillboxes. A portion of this new line went straight on to deal with this pillbox line, and by 9.45 am they were in control – and indeed connected with some men from the 31st who had also come up. Thus what Toll and Purser knew, and what Elliott therefore knew, bore little resemblance as to what was actually happening on the ground. Indeed 5th Divisional Headquarters knew before any of them, as the contact

The left of the Australian attack (4th Division) looking from close to the left of the 5th Division; note the valley between Polygon Wood and the ridge top road leading to Zonnebeke.

ALBANIA WOODS

JOIST FARM   JETTY WARREN

aircraft had seen what was going on and dropped the new position at 11.25 am. This probably saved many lines, as it prevented another barrage being fired at noon, which would undoubtedly have caused severe casualties to the soldiers holding the Blue Line.

The 31st advanced cautiously by use of patrols gradually eating their way towards their goal. They kept in contact with the 29th's right flank, but remained content to let their own right sit in the vicinity of Cameron House, about five hundred yards short of the Blue Line, thereby creating a sharp bend in the line.

Eventually the 33rd Division was in a position to advance; by midday they were on the start line; by 4 pm they had reached the Red Line and by 7 pm had advanced another 150 yards, but were not able to progress beyond the vicinity of Cameron House.

Again this is the story as seen by the 5th's Divisional History, but things were more complex than that. 2/RWF had come up to assist with the assault to bring the 33rd divisional line to its correct position (a more detailed account of whose actions follows after this section). The attack was to be launched at noon, but the barrage was largely ineffectual as it was fired too far to the east, a consequence of the fact that the 98 Brigade commander was unsure of the location of his forward troops, the Argylls. The consequences for the advance were considerable.

> When, about 11 am [noon British time] *the wall of mist on the right flank of the regiment* [230th RIR] *had disappeared, the men of the 230th (on the Polderhoek spur) saw the deploying enemy, behind its rolling barrage, advancing deep on its flank* [ie the 230th right flank] *and manifestly in the act of pushing to the south east. Enemy columns, following after, were trying to reach Polygon Wood. On this incredibly favourable target there now fell at 1,000 - 1,800 metres the fire of all the heavy machine-guns of the regiment that were still available, with annihilating effect, the*

ZONNEBEKE OUT OF SIGHT BEYOND RIDGE

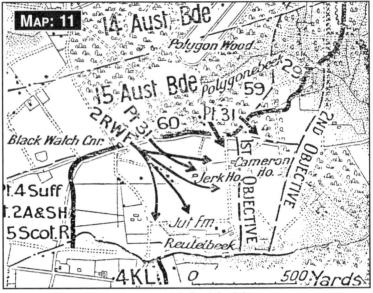

Map showing complications on 15 Brigade's right.

British artillery being unable fully to suppress them. Seven heavy machine-guns of the 1st Company sent streaming out in a short time more than 20,000 rounds.

2/RWF were followed by 'scattered elements' of the 31st, those near Jerk House following the Welshmen as a second wave. The German garrison of that position abandoned it, probably in view of the preparations for the advance towards the house. 2/RWF went beyond Jerk House, but did not get to Cameron House. At this stage ammunition became a problem, a consequence of the destruction by earlier German artillery fire of the painstakingly gathered dumps brought up preparatory to the battle.

At 4 pm line after line of German infantry could be observed advancing over Reutel hill, a kilometre or so away, whilst others were seen to be coming up the Reutelbeek valley, to the right. 2/RWF felt they had no alternative but to fall back in the light of shortage of ammunition; it was agreed that they would come back to Jerk House and the 31st would come back to the First Objective. However the Welshmen did not stop at Jerk House, but continued to fall back, even through the line of the 59th and the 60th. Aerial observation reported that the roads north of Reutel were full of Germans. Corps ordered a barrage to be laid on Hollebosch, a wood to the east of the Broodseinde Ridge, including a large number of gas shells.

With the barrage falling on the Germans, and no apparent pressure

64

on 2/RWF, a number of Australians ran forward to rally the Welshmen. The Germans wilted under the pressure of the artillery fire, and by evening no counter-attack had come close to being able to carry out its function. This was another graphic illustration of the fatal flaw in the German scheme of holding the line lightly and leaving it to counter-attack troops to restore the situation. Before well conducted artillery, such a tactic was doomed to failure.

Elliott, by now considerably impatient, decided to make a personal reconnaissance of his line at 6 am on the 27th. He decided that the final objective was within easy reach and ordered his 60th Battalion (on the right flank in reserve) to take the ground up to the 31st's Blue Line. This was achieved. In fact Marshall's (commanding officer of the 60th) position was entirely within the 33rd Division area. In the afternoon 2/RWF came up on the right – Marshall reported that their advance 'was superb'.

Notwithstanding the enemy barrage and machine-gun fire, they came forward, line after line, in splendid manner.

At long last, by the late afternoon of the 27th, the position had been secured. The last Australian troops came out of the line on 28 September. It is not altogether surprising that the 5th Australian Division decided that the Butte de Polygon would be the most appropriate place to leave their Great War memorial.

Right of the 5th (Australian) Division and the left of the 33rd Division.

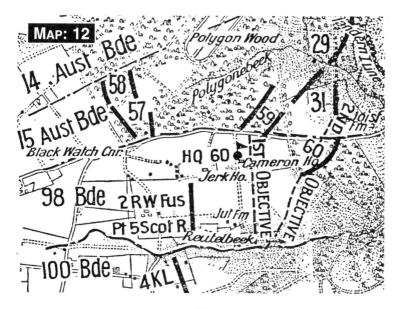

One final loss to the Division at Polygon Wood was Lieutenant-Colonel Humphrey Scott. On being relieved, the commanding officers of the battalions in the line remained twenty four hours to assist their replacements in becoming acquainted with the line. Scott

was showing his successor around he sector on the morning after his battalion had left it when what was apparently a stray bullet, glancing upwards, as was said, from a Tommy's steel helmet, killed instantly both Colonel Scott and Colonel Turnbull, the relieving battalion commander. Perhaps no more gallant or gifted battalion commander than Colonel Scott ever led Australians in the field, and his loss was mourned throughout the whole Division. That night a devoted party of men set out from the 56th Battalion camp and walked many miles through the shelled area to recover the body of their beloved CO and bring it back for burial. They found, however, that these last sad offices had already been carried out by the British troops there, and the body was left on the field near those of the gallant officers and men it had so lately led to victory.

Both Turnbull and Scott were examples of men promoted at an early age. Turnbull, a Gordon Highlander commanding 20/Manchesters, was

29th Australian Battalion building a dug-out on captured ground at Polygon Wood.

only 25 when he was killed; indeed in the middle of September he commanded the brigade in the absence of the Brigadier-General. He was commissioned in 1912, and won his DSO on 13 October 1914, a most unusual award at that date for a subaltern. For some months he commanded 2/Gordons and also served on the staff. He is buried in Buttes New British Cemetery (I.C.9). Scott was only 26. He won his DSO at Gallipoli when a captain.

For conspicuous gallantry in the attack on Lone Pine on 6-7 August 1915. He held on to a very exposed position till all the wounded had been removed. Later, after a heavy bombing attack by superior forces had compelled him to retire, he led a bayonet charge which retook and held a position, in face of the enemy's enfilading machine-gun fire. This position was of great importance as linking up the positions captured on either flank.

Lieutenant-Colonel Scott is also buried in Buttes Cemetery, in II.B.5.

The 4th Division suffered approximately 1450 casualties; the 5th 3,500 and the 33rd 3,500.

2nd Battalion Royal Welch Fusiliers at Polygon Wood.[19]

As an aside, the Royal Welsh Fusiliers were usually known by that name between 1881 and 1920, when the alternative spelling, Welch, was fixed.

The task of the 33rd Division (2/RWF was part of 19 Brigade, of the Division) was to cover the right flank of the Australians in their advance through the remainder of Polygon Wood. The new line would give observation over the Reutelbeek Valley and was essential not only for that task, but future development of the battle around Gheluvelt and across to Polderhoek Chateau.

As explained above, the situation on the 33rd's front was thrown into considerable turmoil by the German counter stroke of 25 September. 2/RWF was transferred to come under the command of 98 Brigade at 8 am on 26 September and was ordered up to the front. By this stage, of course, the Australians had already reached the Red Line. They were to be ready to make an attack at noon on the 26th, in conjunction with the Australians, moving forward from their support position at Stirling Castle, just south of the Menin Road, near Clapham Junction. The move up to the line was to take place at 10 am.

A conference of company commanders was held with Major Roger Poore, commanding the battalion. There were problems, the chief of which was the lack of maps for the company officers. B and D companies were to advance in line towards Polderhoek Chateau, whilst either the support company (A) or the reserve company (C) would

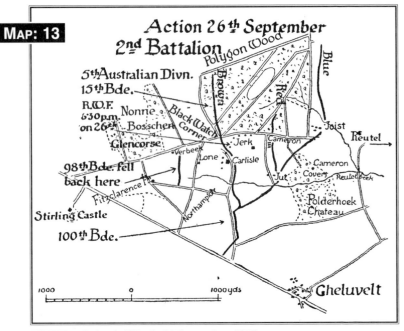

Action 26th September 2nd Battalion

MAP: 13

5th Australian Divn.
15th Bde.

R.O.F.
6.30p.m. Nonne
on 26th. Bosschen

Polygon Wood

Brown

Red

Blue

Joist

Reutel

Glencorse

Black Watch Corner

Verbeek

Jerk

Cameron

98th Bde. fell
back here

Fitzclarence Fm

Lone

Carlisle

Jut

Cameron
Covert

Reutelbeek

Stirling Castle

Northampton

Polderhoek
Chateau

100th Bde.

1000   0   1000yds

Gheluvelt

2/RWF at Polygon Wood, 26 September 1917.

follow, but advance in the direction of Jut Farm, thereby covering the left flank and linking with 15 Brigade of the 5th Australian Division. It was at this conference that the CO was advised by the CO of 11 Field Company RE to take a more circuitous route, actually coming in via the 4th Australian Division's area. The Menin Road was crossed east of Clapham Junction, round the back of Inverness Copse and from there behind Glencorse Wood. The ground was very boggy behind this latter wood,

> the spongy ground and the soft places that had to be jumped caused delay. Soon the track was lined with Lewis gun magazines and rifle grenades cast aside by their carriers.

However this route paid dividends, and there were very few casualties, even when passing through the German barrage between Glencorse Wood and Nonne Boschen. At 11.45 am D Company formed on an east west line with their left close to Black Watch Corner; whilst a couple of platoons of B Company arrived in time to advance with them at zero. The adjutant, Captain Mann, was supervising the jump off, but no sooner had he seen off the remainder of B Company than he was shot through the throat. The advance was made without benefit of any significant artillery cover, as the situation and location of British and Australian troops was so obscure. At about the same time Captain Coster, commanding D Company, was killed as he entered the remnants of the orchard near Jerk Farm. Second Lieutenant Colquhon, commanding B Company was also hit, (buried at Poelcapelle Military Cemetery) and the two companies lost contact– they could not even see each other.

As the various elements of A Company came up, Major Poore ordered them in to the gap he could see being created between B and D; they stuck on to B's left but never made contact with D.

What had happened was that, soon after they set off, D Company changed direction and headed east and collected scattered members of the 31st in their shell holes as they went, and then made their way into a north south trench which lay between Carlisle Farm and Jerk House. Here they took up position, firing at the Germans ahead of them and across the Reutelbeek Valley towards Polderhoek Chateau, which at that time had woods (or remnants of them) surrounding it. It was from here that some of the most effective German fire was coming. B Company came to a halt with its left on Jerk Farm and faced south east. At this stage Battalion Headquarters was entirely ignorant of what the situation might be. A Company eventually ended up as an extension of B, with their right on Lone Farm and their Company Commander, Lloyd Evans, mortally wounded.

Headquarters had taken up a position some 250 yards behind Polygon Wood (ie to the west), and here Poore was to be found awaiting both events and further instructions.

The Medical Officer of the Battalion was the renowned Captain JC Dunn, DSO, MC and Bar, DCM, who after the war compiled what was to become a military classic, *The War the Infantry Knew*, which had a second period as a best seller when it was reprinted in 1987. Dudley Ward's regimental history combines the author's narrative with comments supplied by members of the Battalion, which makes it both an unusual and effective history. The following is a comment made by Dunn of his view of things at about 2.30 pm.

I had had no food since dinner last night, and was going to the Headquarters area, where there was a chance of finding my servant and getting some tea. There the sight of someone drinking stimulated the craving of a young Australian who had been laid down a little way off, and he called out. Because of the nature of his wound I had to refuse him the drink, when a signaller came along and told me that Poore was dead. While he and Casson (Assistant Adjutant) and Colquhoun, who had joined them, were sitting in a shell hole talking, a shell fell on them, killing all three. [And all three are in Poelcapelle Military

69

Cemetery.] *So I went off to look for Radford* [C Company] *to tell him that he was in command.*

At one moment, about 150 yards off, two men suddenly rose into the air, fifteen feet, perhaps, amidst a spout of soil; they rose and fell with the constrained, graceful poise of acrobats; a rifle, revolving slowly, rose high above them before it fell.

He found Radford in a pill box behind B Company at about 3.30 pm, who moved the Headquarters behind B Company to a pill box, in a relatively quiet area. Dunn decided to join him

I was going to join Radford by way of the rifle pit – it was hardly a trench – in which the aid-opost sergeant had settled. The sergeant shouted to me to 'Look out!' amd pointed to a German aeroplane that was only a hundred feet up, or thereby, and as many yards away. 'Get down,' he shouted, ' the – thing has hit me!' It went away, turned over Becelare, and came over us again, amidst a fusillade. It turned again at Lone Farm and crashed on the north side of Polygon Wood. The pilot was found to have been shot. My sergeant showed me the nose of a bullet projecting between two of his ribs in front (I think it had been fired from Polderhoek). He did not realise that it had gone through from his back, and he did not feel ill, but it was to cause septic pneumonia: he died ten days later, close to Beachy Head, where he had played as a boy.

The rest of the day was fairly uneventful. A trench at Carlisle Farm was full of Middlesex dead (from the fighting of 25 September). However, as dusk fell, D Company fell back on the line from which they had been deployed, reporting that the enemy was massing in Polygon Wood and that ammunition was running out. Dunn reports that this decision was made in conjunction with an Australian officer, which ties in with Bean's account, but makes no mention of them being urged back out by Australian soldiers. Certainly A and B companies swung back in line with them , except for two platoons on the extreme right. Supplies were a problem – both food and ammunition; the problem was that everyone who knew about the arrangements had been knocked out of action. Ammunition had to be collected from the dead or from the discarded equipment of the wounded.

Between dark and midnight SOS calls went up from the Reutel direction.

It was a red over green over yellow at that time, a pretty combination of colours over the outline of the trees that was so dark against a midnight sky. Each time the gunners opened on

*their night lines in a frenzy of emulation, and every gun on both
sides fired rapid. The noise was as a rending of our portion of the
firmament. The staccato of the machine-guns filled the intervals
of the larger reports of the shell bursts, and the rush of bullets
through the nearly still air was like the whistling of a cutting
wind. A veil of smoke drifted over us, polluting the freshness of
the autumn night.*

The Battalion was reported to be holding positions about a hundred
yards west of Carlisle Farm, with posts about the same distance from
Jerk Farm. 5/Scottish Rifles were holding a line from the point where
the Brown Line crossed the Reutelbeek to Lone Farm and on to Black
Watch Corner. At dawn Radford went to FitzClarence Farm, where
5/SR had their Headquarters, to try and get orders. A new officer came
up to take over command, and on their return to the line they stopped
at the Australian Headquarters, where Elliott assured them that there
were few Germans in front of their position as he had been to have a
look himself.

A patrol was sent out at 9 am, but did not return until 11.30 am. In
the meantime C and D were sent to occupy the line from which D had
withdrawn the previous evening, whilst 5/SR moved up to Carlisle
Farm and lent 2/RWF a company for the forthcoming advance. Under
pressure from the Australians to get a move on and relieve their anxiety
about their open right flank, the company commanders were
summoned to an orders group in a pill box to the north of Jerk Farm.
Besides advancing, the men were to pick up loose ammunition, as
supplies were still very low. Once more there was to be no artillery
covering fire, as the situation was still unclear. The only bonus to this
situation was that the same applied to the Germans, and they did not
put down any fire either between the Reutelbeek and Polygon Wood
east of Lone Farm.

At 12.30 pm D Company set off, accompanied by D Company of
5/SR, followed by B and C companies, who soon became
intermingled. C Company's right came up to Jut Farm and found it still
held by Germans, but it was rushed on its blind side and fourteen
Germans inside surrendered. The Battalion took its objective, the
sloping ground before Jut Farm, whilst 5/SR occupied the ground to
the south of the farm and took up a line along the Reutelbeek facing
southwards. On that night the men were relieved by elements of the
23rd Division.

Dunn makes some trenchant observations about the Battalion,
noting that Mann, the adjutant, had worked hard in it but that its

71

efficiency was slipping. He also adds a rather caustic comment about coming out from the line.

> *Once clear of the barrage lines, officers were astonished at the strength of their companies. The shell holes in rear had yielded their secrets. During the morning I had remarked to an officer that his company was on a very narrow front. He explained that his strength was only 25: after relief furtive accretions raised the strength of that Company to 60.*

1. Edmonds, Brigadier-General Sir J, *Military Operations France and Belgium* Vol II. HMSO 1948 *(OH)* p. 209

2. Bean, CEW, *The Australian Imperial Force in France 1917,* Angus and Robertson Ltd (Sydney) 1943 *(Bean)*, p.779; p. 790

3. *OH* p.246

4. The planks, chiefly of elm and beech, were about nine feet long, one foot long across and two and a half inches thick. Four or five planks, laid lengthwise (runners) formed the base of the track, and others, laid crosswise and spiked to the runners, formed the surface; half-round pine logs along each edge formed a kerb and kept the wheels on the track. A draining ditch was dug either side of the track, the spoil being used to fill shell holes as necessary.

5. *Bean* p. 764

6. *OH* fn 4 p.257

7. *OH* p. 274

8. Information on this part of the book comes chiefly from, Wyrall, Everard, *The Die-Hards in the Great War Vol II,* 1916 -1919 (London, Harrison and Sons) n.d.

9. *Bean* p. 800. He describes the actions of 25th September and the 26th more fully than found elsewhere pp 799 – 824.

10. *Bean* fn 140, p. 832

11. Anon, *The Fifth Battalion The Cameronians (Scottish Rifles) 1914 – 1919.* Jackson, Son & Co., 1936 p.127. Other extracts are taken from this book, pp 127 – 130.

12. Ellis, Captain AD, *The Story of the Fifth Australian Division.* Hodder and Stoughton, London, n.d. The relevant section is the chapter on Polygon Wood, pp 227 - 256

13. Newton Wanliss, *The History of the Fourteenth Battalion, AIF,* The Arrow Printery, Melbourne, 1929 p. 241. Other extracts are taken from this book.

14. For information on pill boxes in general, I strongly recommend Peter Oldham, *Pill boxes on the Western Front,* Leo Cooper, London 1995. For Polygon Wood in particular see p. 130.

15. For much of this section information has come from *Bean* pp 825-827.

16. Ellis, *op cit* p. 246

17. Stephen Snelling, *VCs of the First World War: Passchendaele 1917*, Alan Sutton 1998 pp 155 – 156. This volume is one of a series covering the VCs of the Great War and is the best published compilation of material on VC winners that is available.

18. *Bean* p. 818.

19. Dudley Ward *op cit*. This section is largely extracted from this regimental history, which records details of the engagement pp 339-348.

Chapter Two

TIGERS HOLD THE LINE

In the middle of August the 21st Division was withdrawn from the line and spent time in a rest area west of Arras. The Leicesters – the 6th, 7th, 8th and 9th battalions (all Kitchener battalions) had been formed into 110 Brigade, originally serving in the 37th Division, but were transferred into the 21st Division after the particularly unfortunate time that that formation had had on 1 July, replacing 63 Brigade. On 16 September the Division was moved up to Flanders, moving by train to the railhead at Caestre. Here more men came to the brigade – for example 7/Leicesters received a draft of 69 men, all of whom had seen service on the Western Front, many of them in the Brigade.

On 26 September 9/Leicesters arrived at Micmac Camp near Ouderdom. The orderly corporal for the battalion was DA Bacon, who kept a full record of events throughout his years with the Leicesters during the Great War. The first problem of which the battalion was

Typical billets behind the lines during Third Ypres; note the summer wear adopted by the soldiers. September was exceptionally hot and dry.

made on arrival at the camp was the danger of aerial bombing.

Here we were warned, and indeed it was very evident, that the enemy made nightly bombing raids by aeroplane [as opposed to Zeppelin]; all the bell tents, of which the camp was formed, had been surrounded by sandbagged walls as a protection therefrom. Strict orders were issued that no lights whatsoever were to be showing after dark, either shaded or otherwise, but as the tents were of white canvas and not even stained dark brown (this was afterwards practised in many cases, and found to be proof against light), it was easier to order than obey. For the troops, perhaps, the condition was not difficult, but for the Orderly Room staff and similarly employed personnel, the strict instructions were impossible. On this night, as on many another, orders reached Battalion HQ well after dusk, and then had to be retyped with various amendments and circulated to Companies. The difficulty of affording a light by which to type, and yet cause none to be seen from without, can readily be imagined, especially when it is borne in mind that the light of a single candle, diffused by a white tent cover, makes an excellent target not only for a particular tent, but for the whole camp. Just as Orders were being drafted, on the ground with the aid of a candle in a biscuit tin under the only table available and with blankets hung all round the tent on the outside, six tremendous bobs dropped and exploded about fifty yards from the camp. The light was out in an instant, and I fear knees rattled, the while the ominous buzz peculiar to German bombing aircraft continued in a manner to make one's blood curdle. The usual 'Hades let loose' followed the first offenders – searchlights swept the skies – 'archies' by the dozen blazed forth and numerous machine-guns specially set for anti-aircraft work joined in the fray. But this was merely the prelude to the Perfect Night! Barely had the 'All Clear' been sounded, and the Orders again commenced, than a second addition arrived; and the alternate quiet and infernal noise continued until dawn, and what is more continued more or less every night until the signing of the Armistice.

On 29 September the Brigade marched to Dickebusch and bivouacked in Scottish Wood.

The camp was some five miles from the then present Front Line and lay to the eastern edge of Dickebusch Lake. Very heavy firing was in progress, and as the line of the heavies was now reached, the noise was deafening; by night, in the light of either

*the moon or stars, the lake presented an excellent target for the
enemy aircraft, of which they took full advantage.*

The Brigade was to move up o the line on 30 September. The first part
of the journey took them up to Zillebeke Lake, where the two front
battalions, the 7th and 8th, had tea. They marched in Battle Order. At
the lake they received also the decorations that made them look like
Christmas trees – picks and shovels for all ranks, grenades, mortar
bombs and extra ammunition for the machine-guns and themselves.

*From this point forward all was devastation; the ground was
riddled with shell holes (near Zillebeke itself they were mostly
old ones), and of trees nothing but the stumps remained. The only
buildings to be seen were the ruins of Ypres to the west. The
Ypres-Messines canal, which had been crossed on the march up,
was damned up and wooden bridges had replaced those blown
up in 1914. The railway was blown up, torn up and hopelessly
destroyed. A more dreary and abandoned vista could not readily
be imagined – the normal face of the country was obliterated,
and the once tranquil village of Zillebeke was levelled with the
earth. The only form of life was provided by the continuous
stream of the British war machine, the roar of the guns, and the
smoking vibrations of the bursting shells and, aloft, the
numerous kite balloons scanning the horizon. Such was the*

**Members of the Tigers' Brigade resting in a support trench on the way to
the line.**

prospect, and it was by no means improved on acquaintance.
Having been burdened with the necessaries for holding a position, the Leicesters made their way to the ground that had been captured on 26 September.

The route led by a much broken road to Hooge Crater, thence across the Ypres-Menin road, where a sleeper track was encountered. This track was laid, or rather embedded, in mud ranging from three to six feet deep, and pursued its course through Glencorse Wood whence the track, now narrowed to one eighteen inches in width and continued via Black Watch Corner to Polygon Wood. The narrow portion consisted of duckboards

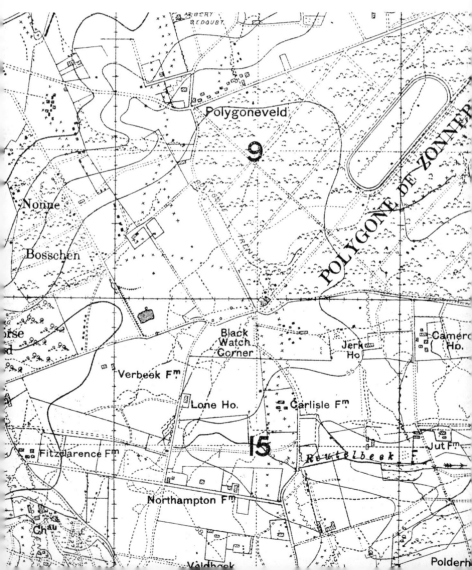

(slats of wood 3î x 18î placed every three inches on longitudinal battens underneath). He night was very dark and the track broken in many places by shell fire, moreover it was exceedingly slippery owing to recent rains and the mud; and the passage of the tracks was painfully slow and laborious, especially as everyone was fully laden with war accoutrements.

The relief was completed by about 10.30 pm, the 9th on the right, the 8th on the left, with 1/RWF to the left of 8/Leicesters and the 23rd Division (70 Brigade) on the right of 9/Leicesters. 7/Leicesters were in support in dugouts near Black Watch Corner. This battalion went into the line with 19 officers and 400 other ranks, which gives some

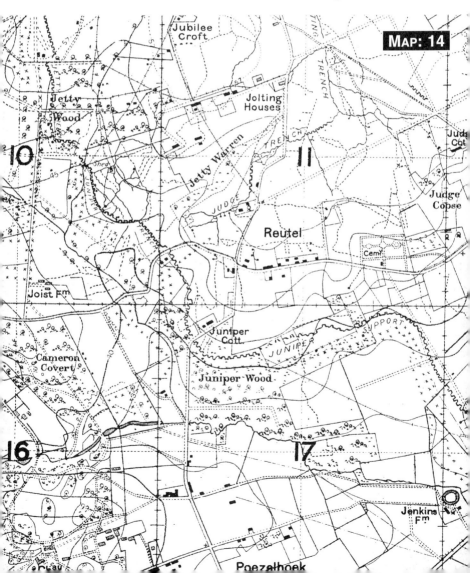

indication of the understrength nature of the brigade as a whole. The men were disposed as follows: C Company (right front) at J.9.d.2.1; D Company (left front) at J.9.d.2.7; B Company (support) at J.9.c.9.1 and A Company (reserve) at J.9.c.1.1; with Battalion Headquarters at J.14.b.7.8. The front companies had the basics of dug positions within which they could take shelter; the others had to dig in – but the whole relief was carried out without a single casualty.

6/Leicesters were in reserve at Railway Dugouts near Zillebeke Lake. Behind the position of 8/Leicesters was the Butte, under which a Canadian Tunnelling Company was hard at work, reopening blown in entrances and strengthening the works.

Jack Horner served in the 8th, 1st and 6th Leicesters from the time that he enlisted in March 1915 to the time that he was severely wounded in October 1917 (although he was not finally discharged until August 1918). It was my privilege to interview him in 1982 when I was writing a series of articles for a special supplement that the *Leicester Mercury* was producing, entitled *Bygone Leicestershire*. He was one of fifteen or so veterans who served in 6, 7, 8 and 9/Leicesters, together forming 110 (Leicesters) Brigade with whom I spent time discussing their Great War service.

Jack was badly wounded near Polygon Wood, on his way up to the line. He suffered for the rest of his life from that wound - indeed his left arm became permanently shorter than his right. His wartime experience left him bitter, but his recollections of his time in the army were also sweet - the comradeship and many of the experiences were

Photograph taken before the Third Battle of Ypres commenced.

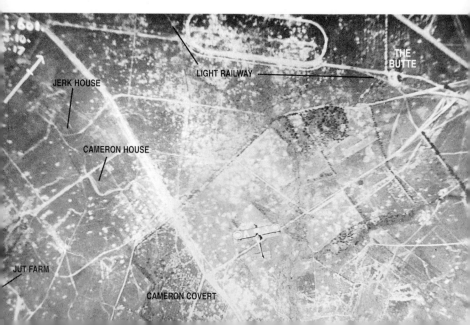

sources of pride and enjoyment. Perhaps it would be more accurate to say that events following his wounding and the treatment that he and so many like him received in the post war period left him bitter.

September 26th 1917. Go to Dickebush by lorries. This is the first time - and only time - we've been moved by transport; whatever is this man's army coming to!? Such pampering! However we did in a couple of hours what would have been a hard day marching, and that's really something.

We are very near the Menin Road, quite a way from Wipers, where there has been some very heavy fighting, and you can see the result of that all round you, the terrain pockmarked with shell holes; the mud ankle-deep; a tank lying at a grotesque angle near the road. The Germans had excavated underneath the Menin Road and made a very good dugout with bunks and plenty of space and quick ways to get outside. They must have done that when the tanks came charging along. We were allowed to go inside and have a look around, on very strict orders not to touch anything, as they might be booby traps.

September 29 1917. Battle Orders coming through, two battalions to go into the line tomorrow, 30th; 6th and 8th are in support, 7th and 9th are in the advance with C Company of the 6th in support of the 9th for the attack. This is a very short statement of fact, but what really happened to all of us is very different.

Actually it is not a statement of fact – the Leicesters Brigade was merely going to hold the line in preparation for an attack to be made

Looking at Polygon Wood from the north.

by 62 and 64 Brigades. 6/Leicesters were in reserve well behind, 8/Leicesters were in the front, not 7/Leicesters, 7/Leicesters were support to 9/Leicesters, not 6/Leicesters. What all this illustrates is the potential limitation of oral evidence, in this case as regards events surrounding large units, such as battalions. On the other hand, the clear account of what happened to an individual is enormously powerful, bringing home to those who have no concept of the reality of conflict something of what these men had to endure.

The whole area, many square miles of it, is really a sea of mud, caused by intense shelling, which destroyed the drainage system, and the result was a thick, gluey mud, ankle - at times thigh - deep, difficult to move through.

The shelling was not very heavy, compared with what I had experienced before, but the jagged fragments of iron and steel from an exploding shell can travel hundreds of yards with the speed of an express train, and when they hit they smashed through flesh and bone to cause horrible wounds.

My company, A, was moving up in single file in support of the 9th Battalion when from nowhere (I don't remember seeing or hearing any shelling) a piece of shrapnel hit my left forearm, I was knocked flat, and when I came round I was alone, with a smashed arm. I gripped my arm above the elbow with my right hand to strop the blood flow, and somehow got my arm laying across my stomach, the blood soaking my tunic. (My Diary is by

Orgainised chaos surrounded the evacuation of the wounded. This is a scene on the Menin Road, near Birr Cross Road.

my side now, though faded, it was written in 1917, is now dog-
eared, and still shows the blood stains.) [It is now in the Imperial
War Museum.]

I stumbled on, I don't know how and God knows where,
through the mud and slime, over a great sea of mud; no idea
where I was or were I was going or how long I had been
stumbling around, for I saw no-one and in all this space no-one
saw me. Honestly, I have no recollection whatever of these
wanderings.

It was dusk, or maybe night time, when I saw a chink of light
some distance away and made for it as best I could. It was a
German pillbox. I went in and again almost faded out, but thank
Heaven they were British, using the pillbox as an advanced
dressing station and for stretcher bearers and other medical
orderlies.

I asked for water (I can still taste petrol in that water now),
they asked me where the hell I came from, and I couldn't tell
them, I was all in, but they knew from my shoulder flashes what
division I came from, and that was miles away.

It is worth pointing out that both water and petrol was delivered in the
same metal cans, the only difference being the colour of the cap. This
obviously made it relatively easy for the two to get mixed up, so
Horner's water had been polluted by the petrol which had been in the
container previously.

I was weary, exhausted, wet though and covered in mud; they
made me, and many others, as comfortable as possible as the
circumstances permitted, and waited for the ambulances to come
up the line. We waited many hours, how long I don't know, I was
all in and about out, very very tired and I have not much
recollection of where I was. Eventually the ambulances came, I
don't remember whether they were horse drawn of motors, but it
was the most painful and horrible journey that I have ever made.
With every lurch and bump the smashed bones were digging into
the raw flesh, it was a nightmare journey.

Jack Horner wrote up his memories as *Memoirs of a Trench Rat*; it is
quite clear that his last years saw him casting his mind back to those
fraught years, between the ages of 17 and 20, when he was a member
of the army, and all that he then experienced. At the age of nineteen and
a half he was to be maimed and disabled for the rest of his life.

The night was quite quiet; at headquarters of 9/Leicesters, in a
mebus *(Mannschafts Eisenbeton Understände)* – better known to

British troops as a pill box – the men were ordered to rest whilst they could. The bunker was a small one, and only accommodated the officers; the rest took possession of a number of shell holes in the immediate vicinity. Once orders had been given out an attempt was made to settle down for the remnant of the night.

> *...we were mud-wallowing in the open air, it was bitterly cold and no blankets could have been brought, and we were on the edge of a volcano that might, and as a matter of fact did, belch forth at any moment. First we dug ourselves in as well as possible, in front of the Headquarter Mebus, and with the aid of some old planks lying about, contrived to make a little shelter and a firing position. At about midnight we lay down in the mud with the idea of sleeping, each one taking turn at sentry.*
>
> *About 5 am we were rudely awakened by a terrific barrage, supplied by the enemy, and which was later shown to have covered the whole immediate front to a depth of some thousand yards* [the barrage covered the fronts of the 23rd Division, north of the Reutelbeek, the 21st and the 7th] *and it is no exaggeration to say that the shells burst as thick as a hailstorm, and the din was awful. Tree stumps, mud and everything that happened to be about was going up in all directions.*

The Germans also lay down a smoke barrage, so that useful observation was impossible; fortunately the German barrage coincided

Polygon Wood and the Butte.

with a British so-called practice barrage – heavy barrages laid regularly along the front designed to confuse the Germans as to when a full scale British attack was going to happen. In fact the British barrage could not be heard, so loud was the cacophony of noise created by the German fire, but shell bursts could be seen through the smoke on the German side of the line.

That he did not, even in the first few minutes, let alone throughout the assault, hit the Headquarters position [J.10.c.1.2] was nothing short of miraculous, and every moment was awaited as the last. Dawn was breaking, and at 5.15 am enemy planes flew low over our lines, so low in fact that the occupants could be seen quite plainly, the while they fired drum after drum of machine-gun bullets into the troops.

On the left front was 8/Leicesters; adjacent to them was 1/RWF (Royal Welsh [Welch] Fusiliers), who occupied Jetty Trench, part of the Flanders I line, to the east of the northern part of Polygon Wood. With its right rather to the south of Jetty Wood. 1/RWF had had a rather unusual time in mid-September when they were whisked off at short notice to Etaples, the huge base area, to quell a mutiny (the one involving, so it is said, the infamous Monocled Mutineer).

They arrived at midnight on 13 September and found, as war reports read, 'the situation well in hand'. In the afternoon of the

Philip Bent.

14th, C Company mounted guard over the Field Prisoners Compound, while the rest of the battalion 'stood to'. A display of discipline put an end to the disturbance, and on the 17th the battalion, having enjoyed a breath of sea-air and a swim in sea-water, entrained once more for the battle front.

The attack fell on this part of the front soon after 6 am. D Company held the right front, and it was this part that was most threatened, though by 7am the enemy had been driven off.

The Germans had advanced in three waves, and had almost reached our trenches before the first wave was wiped out by our rifle and machine-gun fire; the succeeding waves hesitated, and commenced to retire. D Company, reinforced by two platoons from A (the support company) immediately left their trench and advanced on the wavering Germans, drove them back into our artillery barrage, captured four, and also drove the garrison from a pill-box, which they occupied, appropriating a machine-gun the enemy had abandoned.

This illustrates the significance of the machine-gun to German fighting capability. The numbers of guns in each battalion increased dramatically as the war progressed.

In fact, so successful was the counter-attack that it was possible that the battalion could have moved forward to capture the ridge before them, but the confusion on the right and the situation within the 21st Division meant that this thought had to be abandoned.

The German artillery barrage was also being fired in enfilade at the right flank of this front, as the Germans still held their positions around Polderhoek Chateau and in Gheluvelt beyond.

The worst of the attack was to fall on the boundary between 9/Leicesters and the 23rd Division – the area that had caused so much of a problem just a couple of days earlier – in the vicinity of Joist Farm.

> *At 5.30 am the enemy launched a determined assault against our positions under cover of the smoke screen. The first wave of attackers was beaten off by A Company [this was the right front company], using Lewis gun and rifle fire. The second wave was also successfully driven off on the Brigade Front, but penetrated somewhat into the lines of the battalion on our left flank. By this time the SOS was being sent up all along the front – several were discharged at Headquarters, both night and daylight rockets – and the situation looked threatening; Brigade Headquarters was called upon for immediate help. Under the determined pressure of the enemy A Company commenced, and continued, to fall back. Lieutenant-Colonel PE Bent DSO, commanding 9th Leicesters, decided to make a counter-attack with such forces as were available, as no help could be expected from the troops in support for some hours, owing to the conditions of approach and the deep and heavy enemy barrage. Collecting together all men of the Headquarters and the company in Battalion support, the Colonel lead the charge shouting, 'Come on the Tigers'.*

This attack was launched at 5.40 am. The men he gathered together were two platoons of D Company, who were in reserve from J.10.c.1.3 to J.10.c.1.1 and B Company, who were in support from J.10.c.6.4 to J.10.c.6.0 along with member of his Headquarters.

> *This gallant attempt was, for the moment, entirely successful, though Colonel Bent was shot through the temple whilst leading his men.*

Philip Bent received his DSO in the Birthday Honours in June 1917 – his rank given as Second Lieutenant (Temporary Major, acting Lieutenant-Colonel). Although born in Canada (in 1891), in Halifax, Nova Scotia, he was educated in England, having come back to the country with his mother. At the age of 17 he decided to join the Merchant Navy, rather interestingly, as his home town of Ashby de la

Zouch could not be much further from the sea. He joined the army as a private in October 1914 (another career change – why not the navy?), but was commissioned into the Leicesters and stayed with either the 7th or 9th Leicesters for his entire military career. He enjoyed military life from the start, and was able to gain a regular commission in due course.

The London Gazette of 11 January 1918 published his VC.

Philip Eric Bent DSO, Second Lieutenant (Temporary Lieutenant-Colonel), Leicestershire Regiment. For most conspicuous bravery when, during a heavy hostile attack, the right of his own command and the battalion on his right were forced back. The situation was critical owing to the confusion caused by the attack and the intense artillery fire. Lieutenant-Colonel Bent personally collected a platoon that was in reserve and together with men from other companies and various regimental details, he organised and led them forward to the counter-attack, after issuing orders to other officers as to the further defence of the line.

The counter-attack was successful and the enemy were [sic]checked. The coolness and magnificent example shown to all ranks by Lieutenant-Colonel Bent resulted in the securing of a portion of the line which was of essential importance for further operations.

His mother collected his DSO and his VC at an investiture at Buckingham Palace in the spring of 1918. Bent's body was never found, and this extraordinary 26 year old soldier is commemorated on the Tyne Cot Memorial.

Lieutenant-Colonel Bent's place was taken by the senior company commander, Captain Drew of C Company, who ordered that no retirement was to be made and that every man would have to fight to the last.

The enemy continued, however, to advance on the right and launched a third wave against our own front; another counter-attack was organised and further progress by the enemy was checked on the Brigade front.

This assault was launched by two platoons of C Company; another two platoons were sent off to reinforce – and to make contact with – the troops on the right flank, who had been driven back some distance.

As a result of the heavy casualties already sustained by the Battalion, the front posts were withdrawn about a hundred yards on the right, and a defensive flank organised.

Tanks stuck near the Menin Road.

A defensive line was formed approximately a hundred yards behind the front line, approximately along the eastern edge of Polygon Wood; C Company established a defensive flank from J.10.c.6.0 in front of Cameron House to J.16.a.2.7. Contact was still lost with troops on the right flank.

This was about 9 am, and in a much exhausted and disordered condition a few of the 7th Leicesters began to arrive. It appeared that they had been terribly cut up in coming to our aid, having been literally scattered in all directions; fully half of their effectives had been knocked out, and the rest, distracted but

welcome, arrived too late to have been of service if the initial
onslaughts of the enemy had been successful.

The Germans kept up a very heavy artillery barrage on the track from the west end of Polygon Wood and the road between Black Watch Corner and Glencorse Wood. The two companies of 7/Leicesters that eventually made it were reduced to about seventy men.

The CO of 7/Leicesters took over command, keeping the 9th in the front and using the men of the 7th as support troops, close up.

Touch had been maintained throughout with the 8th Battalion on the left, despite the extreme difficulty owing to the fierce fighting, and the very marshy nature [the Polygonbeek flowed out of their part of the line] *of the low lying ground on that flank. After 10 am the situation settled down to a fierce artillery duel, though the enemy snipers continued to be most active, as also their aircraft. The latter, on this occasion, must have helped the enemy considerably during the assault, as their crews provided not only additional covering fire, but shouted encouragements to their men.*

Tension continued for the remainder of the day; artillery duels broke out periodically, whilst a further German attempt to launch an attack from the cover of Cameron Covert was brought to a premature halt by a hurricane of artillery and machine-gun fire. An enemy aircraft, flying at about two hundred feet, was brought down by ground fire at about 10.30 am, landing in No Man's Land, where it and the crew were destroyed by shell fire.

The night, apart from the extreme violence of the artillery, passed quietly; every man 'stood to' and took turns in strengthening the defences, burying the dead and carrying out the wounded. The latter work was laborious, tedious and dangerous in the extreme, owing to the restricted lines of communication, the darkness and the incomparable hardships of the tracks. It was a perilous journey of five or six hours for a stretcher party, which having discharged their load, returned for more. No trace was found either during the night or afterwards of the body of the Colonel, though thorough searches were made.

At one stage, at 11 pm, the SOS signal went up from both right and left flanks, and a deafening defensive artillery barrage came down; the Germans fired literally thousands of Very lights, but otherwise took very little action. During the day the War Diary reported that the men had 'good shooting' as Germans who were left behind in the attack tried to get back to their own lines.

To the right of 110 Brigade was 69 Brigade of the 23rd Division. They had come into the line rather earlier than the Leicesters, for the 33rd Division, after its exhausting time on 26 and 27 September, had to be relieved. The 23rd Division was recalled to the front after only a couple of days rest. The front was to be held by 70 Brigade (right) and 69 Brigade (left), whilst 68 Brigade was in support, though based well back at Westoutre, with two battalions in Ridge Wood, just south east of Dickebusch Lake; this had the advantage that it was well beyond German artillery fire, so that at least they would be reprieved from that particular ordeal, if not from aerial bombardment.

The right part of the Divisional front extended from the Menin Road to a point about 450 yards due east of Northampton Farm. The right brigade held the line with three companies of 8/Yorkshire (the Green Howards), with a reserve company spread out from the vicinity of Black Watch Corner to Carlisle Farm. 11/West Yorks was in support in an area north of Inverness Copse and 9/Yorkshire, in the north-eastern quarter of Sanctuary Wood, was also available for support.

During the night of 28 September the 5th Australia Division withdrew from its extension into the area of the 33rd Division, and a company of 9/Yorkshire was brought in to take their place, taking over that part of Cameron Covert in British possession and the line to its immediate north. Although there was no major German activity during this time, still it was far from quiet – for example a very heavy German barrage around Black Watch Corner, which killed 25 men in 8/Yorkshire and wounded 15 others. Attacks were made in some strength, in particular on 70 Brigade front. On the morning of 30 September this involved an attack with flamenwerfer and German infantry who had managed to get up to the front line under cover of a stiff artillery barrage, smoke, and most helpfully, an early morning mist. They achieved nothing. On the night of 30 September/1 October, 8/Yorkshire was relieved by the rest of 9/Yorkshire (their C Company retaining its position on the extreme left) and a company of 10/Duke of Wellington's. At this time 110 Brigade came in to replace the Australians; to the right of C Company was the company of Duke's men. That same night the Pioneers of the 33rd Division completed a much needed communication trench from FitzClarence Farm (close to 9/Yorkshire HQ) to within a short distance of Carlisle Farm via Lone House.

The artillery barrage hit 69 Brigade hard, including in enfilade on the north bank of the Reutelbeek, and on a line south of Black Watch Corner.

From the first, communcation between battalion headquarters and the front line was impossible. All wires were immediately cut; dust and smoke prevented visual signalling; no runner could pass alive through the hail of bursting shells. Pigeons were released, in the hope that these at least might carry back reports, but they alike failed. [In fact a number of these were killed by concussion.][2]

C Company, 9/Yorkshire and D Company the Duke's occupied the front line running from Cameron Covert down to the Reutelbeek, but it was on a spur, and therefore concealed from view from almost all other parts of the brigade. Early on in the fighting the position came under attack from waves of Germans coming from the north and the south, trying to pinch out this salient into their ground. Just north of Cameron Covert two Lewis guns were almost immediately put out of action. As men of 9/Leicesters began to give way under the pressure of further assaults, so the men of the Green Howards also fell back, some fifty yards, and then prepared to counter-attack. Unfortunately both the officers involved in the action were both hit, and almost the same time the Germans launched another wave, which meant that the line had to fall back a further 150 yards to ensure that the position was not entirely enveloped.

To the south resolute action was taken by Second Lieutenant Lewis, who with a bombing party managed to retrieve a captured Lewis gun and removed the Germans from the trench to his left; but in the process he was killed by a sniper. Meanwhile the Duke of Wellington's also faced attacks in their position in the marshy area to the south, holding the line by means of a series of shell holes; the Germans got nowhere and eventually abandoned their efforts, contenting themselves with digging in behind some old German wire.

At the end of the day, and despite the most ferocious shelling, especially of the support and reserve lines and the headquarters positions, the 23rd Division had given way only on the extreme left, on a front of about 200 yards and to approximately a similar depth.

On the 21st Division front 7/9 Leicesters were relieved at 10 pm on 2 October, and moved out to the camp at Scottish Wood.

The outgoing was worse, if such degrees could be gauged, than the entry, for the track was heavily shelled with gas shells, forcing one to adjust the mask. The feeling of horror on the narrow slippery track, surrounded by three or four feet of liquid mud, in the awful darkness rendered by the addition of gas helmets, and amid the continuous shelling of the only way out, can be neither described nor imagined by any who were sufficiently fortunate to escape that experience. The continuity of the track was broken at frequent intervals and one hopelessly floundered to regain it. Often refuge had to be taken in one of the Mebusses dotted about, owing to a sudden fierceness or directness of the shelling, but the occasion was but a respite, as by waiting for the shelling to cease one would never have got through at all.

The rendezvous was between Railway Dugouts and Zillebeke Lake, where tea awaited the soldiers as they straggled in, having been instructed on relief to make their own way back to the rendezvous, doing so as a body being adjudged too dangerous. The men of the joint battalion eventually reached Scottish Wood at 3 am, utterly exhausted.

The brigade was reorganised, temporarily, into a three battalion formation; the 8th and the 9th, the two front line battalions, were amalgamated into one; 7/Leicesters was reduced to two strong platoons and a large Lewis gun section per company, whilst only 6/Leicesters emerged relatively unscathed.

German attacks to disturb the next phase in Plumer's stage by stage advance on the Passchendaele and Broodseinde ridges had failed.

1. CH Dudley Ward SO MC, Regimental Records of the Royal Welch Fusiliers, Vol III 1914-1918 France and Flanders. London, Foster Groom and Co Ltd., 1928. p 353.
2. HR Sandilands CMG DSO, The 23rd Division 1914-1919. William Blackwood and Sons, London, 1925, p. 200. Further details on the attack is generally taken from this work.

Plank tracks were the only relatively safe way of moving around the battlefield.

Chapter Three

THE FLANK GUARD FOR THE BATTLE OF BROODSEINDE

4th October 1917

The task of X Corps (which had, from the right, the 7th, the 21st and the 5th divisions in the line) was to continue the advance towards the eastern edge of the Gheluvelt Plateau and act as a right flank guard for the continuing push to the Broodseinde Ridge and beyond to the north. This meant that it had to continue the push eastwards but at the same time protect the left flank as the salient into the German lines was pushed further and further forward. Thus the 7th had as its first objective the Reutel-Broodseinde track and from there on to the ridge road, an advance of only a little short of a mile. This they achieved, so that the two advancing brigades were in a position to look across the Heulebeek depression and into the green lands undamaged by warfare of the German rear areas. The 21st Division was to occupy the high ground above the Reutelbeek valley, across which was the spur on which Polderhoek Chateau stood. For this attack they were to be

Battle of Broodseinde: The right flank.

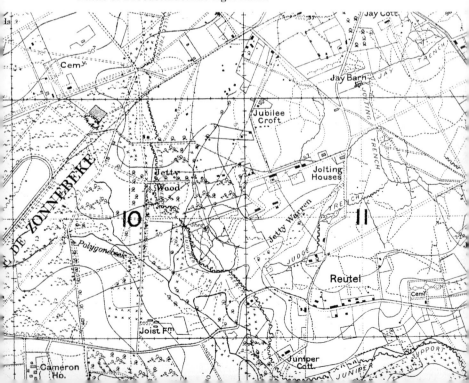

assisted by four tanks, and this battle was to result in the first award of a VC to a member of the fledgling Tank Corps. Although not all objectives were gained, after prolonged and heavy fighting a secure flank was established. The 5th Division managed to clear, at long last, Cameron Covert, which had been a chief means whereby counter-attack troops had been able to enter the Polygon Wood sector and cause so much trouble to Imperial and Australian divisions in the previous fortnight. They were rather less successful in the assault on the Polderhoek spur, and only just managed to retain a footing in the park to the west of the chateau. Failure here was put down to the fact that there was no whole-hearted simultaneous assault on Gheluvelt, the action taking place almost entirely to the north of the Menin Road. Operations against Gheluvelt Wood and Tower Hamlets by the 37th Division (of IX Corps) were carried out, but achieved negligible results.

Because not all objectives were taken on the 4th, the battle in this sector dragged on for several days after 4 October. The next major operation, on 9 October, is known as the Battle of Poelcapelle, and although fighting continued on the front which concerns this guide, it is difficult to see it as anything other than a subsidiary, clearing-up operation.

4 October was described in a German official monograph, *Flandern 1917*, as 'the black day of October 4th'. The catastrophe to German

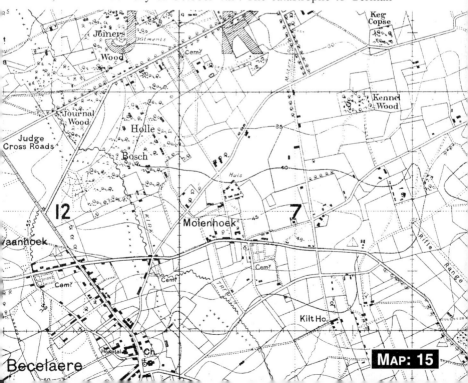

arms was the consequence of two factors. Further to the north east (though this did include part of the 7th Division's front) the Germans had planned a counter-stroke of their own. However, the British barrage forestalled theirs by some ten minutes, and the result was that the assaulting troops were hammered by a fierce British barrage with devastating consequences. The British and Anzac troops captured over 4,000 prisoners on the Second Army front alone. The German 45th Reserve Division lost 83 officers and 2,800 other ranks, and the 4th Guard Division 86 officers and 2,700 other ranks – which figure does not include the lightly wounded who returned to duty after a short spell.

The second reason is summarised by Ludendorff is his *My War Memories* 1914-1918.

> *The battle on the 4th October was extraordinarily severe, and again we only came through it with enormous losses. It was evident that the idea of holding the front line more densely, adopted at my last visit to the front in September, was not the remedy.*

German prisoners being escorted along the Menin Road, passing troops moving up to the front.

The German Official Account for this period was not published until 1942, and then only for a limited and restricted circulation. The British did not get sight of this until 1946, when its own, often subsequently challenged, version of events had not been published, the whole Third Ypres campaign by this stage having become highly controversial. Thus the German account notes that

> *The new Lossberg battle scheme had not stood the test on the 4th October.*

The commander of the Fourth Army ordered (on advice from Ludendorff, given the previous day) his subordinate commanders on 7 October that

> *The foremost line of shell craters, if no natural obstacle was available, to be occupied by a quite thin screen of posts with light machine-guns. A main line of resistance was to be constructed 500 to 600 yards behind this screen*

This was a not very happy compromise of the Somme approach – well manned forward positions, the ground to be defended to the last man, and the Eingreif strategy, of keeping counterattack divisions in the rear to launch counter-strokes. These Eingreif (which actually translates as interlocking) divisions were allocated, at least initially, on the basis of one to every two front line divisions. These could be called upon if a Second Line was breached and would come under the command of the front line divisional commander.

The situation caused by Third Ypres to the German army is encapsulated in comments made by General Herman von Kuhl, Rupprecht's highly respected Chief of the General Staff, in his two volume book Der Weltkrieg 1914-1918.

This supply of reinforcements was bound to become even more difficult in the ensuing years, so that in the end the conduct of the war was definitely influenced by it. On this point Field Marshal Haig has been quite right: if he did not actually break through the German front, the Flanders battle consumed the German strength to such a degree that the harm done could no longer be repaired. The sharp edge of the German sword had become jagged.

Another German general, Moser, who fought against the British at Cambrai, wrote,

In millions of letters from the Western Front from April to November came the ever-rising bitter complaints of the almost unbearable losses in the scarcely interrupted chain of battles: Arras, Aisne-Champagne [the Nivelle offensive], *Flanders* [Third Ypres], *Verdun and the Chemin des Dames* [Malmaison]. *A hundred thousand leave men told the Home Front by word of mouth the details of the ever-growing superiority of the enemy, particularly in weapons of destruction.*

This is not to say that the British army felt filled with optimism and enthusiasm as Third Ypres dragged on – far from it. But is does illustrate a fact that the German army was suffering from deficiencies in its munitions and the calibre of its infantry (in this latter case, so were the British and French). It meant that no longer could the German effort on the Western Front remain dependent on a policy of aggressive defence and security behind lines of wire and concrete fortifications. Bring enough artillery to bear and these would disintegrate under the storm of fire; whilst counter-attacks would collapse under the hail of the protecting artillery barrage that was set up on the newly captured line. An alternative had to be found, and with the virtual collapse of Russia and the arrival of the Americans in overwhelming numbers by 1919, it was perceived that there was little alternative but to engage in the series of ultimately disastrous offensives in which the German army was engaged in 1918.

This introduction, putting Third Ypres in a wider perspective, is included because it is all too dangerous in the Great War to see a particular battle as an end in itself. Very often one is overcome by the tragedy that fell particular units or individuals. On the other hand it is important to understand what the forces were that fell upon those at senior command level – both political and military – in order to appreciate the why, even if some might consider this to be an inadequate justification for the carnage and squalor that characterised much of what took place in 1917.

The 7th Division

The last major fighting in which this Division had been engaged was at Bullecourt in May, though this is not to say that it had not suffered casualties which were known, in a dreadfully accurate way, as 'trench wastage'. In mid August they moved well behind the line for training and rest, which lasted for some six weeks. The Divisional history records the type of training that was undertaken:

> *There was much that was novel in the training through which the Division was now being put. Special attention was paid to musketry, an effort being made to work up to a 12 aimed rounds a minute standard* [compared with the pre-war Regular army's 15 aimed rounds a minute], *the men being taught to look upon the rifle and bayonet as their principal weapons and to regard the bomb and the rifle grenade as supplementary.*

The 7th Division Memorial to the fighting of 1914 and 1917 on Broodseinde Ridge.

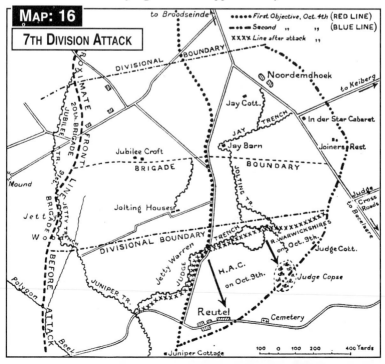

This had become an important issue within the army; there had been a growing tendency to find the solution to all problems on the ground in the grenade, whilst marksmanship had seriously declined.

> *Firing from the hip whilst advancing was also practised, more with the idea of keeping down the enemy's fire during the advance than inflicting casualties. Special importance was attached to the co-ordination of the different weapons in attacks on isolated strong points or on snipers and machine-guns in shell-holes. The progress of the offensive at Ypres was making it clear that the Germans were adopting new methods of defence. German orders had been captured which laid down the new principles, inculcating less rigid methods and in particular the abandonment of formal trench lines in favour of nests of shell-holes linked up by tunnels and covered by wire which, though practically continuous, was to be irregular in trace so as to make the attackers change direction and come under enfilade fire. Deep dug-outs in the first and second lines were to be abandoned as having proved mere man-traps, reserves were now to be posted some little way behind, taking advantage of any facilities for concealment like woods or ravines. Indeed most of the defending infantry was to be kept out of the forward zone, the defence of which was mainly entrusted to machine-guns at irregular intervals, usually either in pill-boxes or in shell-holes. There was to be a continuous support line* [in the case of the Polygon Wood sector, the Flanders I Line], *but sited a mile or so back behind the zone of fortified shell-holes.*

The view is from the Menin road and shows the planked by-pass near Birr Cross-road, trucks on the light railway leading north of Bellewaarde Lake, a duckboard track, and a party of the 56th Battalion AIF making, under supervision of the 14th Field Company with pioneers, a planked siding for the Birr Cross engineer dump.

The Division also received reinforcements, 91 and 20 brigades between them getting over 2,100 men, quite good in both quality and physique as they were drawn from broken up Second Line Yeomanry and Territorial formations or Cyclist battalions in the United Kingdom. This raised the paper strength of a battalion to a thousand men, though courses, leave, sickness and trench wastage rapidly reduced that to about 800.

On 30 September the 7th Division moved to the line previously occupied by the 4th Australian Division, and its headquarters were established at Chateau Segard. The front line position was not far from that in which the Division fought at First Ypres, in 1914; and so, understandably, one of the Divisional Memorials was placed on Broodseinde Ridge after the war. The part played by the Division's right in the German counter-stroke of 1 October has been covered in the preceding chapter.

For the attack on 4 October, 91 Brigade covered the right of the divisional attack. The Division's first objective was the Red Line, 400 yards or so short of the Broodseinde-Becelaere road, on the Reutel track; the second was the Blue Line which would take them some yards over the main ridge road.

91 Brigade was to use 1/South Staffords to take the Red Line, whilst 22/Manchesters was to spearhead the attack on the Blue Line, with 21/Manchesters as support and 2/Queen's in reserve.

The forming up line was about fifty yards to the rear of the forward posts in Jubilee and Jetty trenches; each brigade had a frontage of about five hundred yards. The assaulting battalions for the first objective occupied a depth of some 120 yards and the supporting battalions were 200 yards further behind that. The barrage was designed to be quite slow to take into account the difficulty of moving over the ground, which was just as well as rain started just before zero, making the ground treacherously slippery. Once the Red Line was captured the barrage was to protect the line for an hour and a half to allow for reorganisation, and then advance to an even slower rate so that the Blue Line should be occupied three hours after the troops had set off, that is by 9 am.

About an hour before zero a German defensive barrage had come down; it fell between the front line ad the supports and did little damage – the attacking battalions just brought their rear men forward. And then the attack began.

The British barrage gave the attacking battalions the greatest possible satisfaction: it was accurate, regular, and most effective,

while its slow pace allowed the infantry to keep well up with it.
... The Germans were in unusual strength but proved strangely
ready to surrender: 8/Devons [on the left] *took over 200*
prisoners without having half that number of casualties. 1/South
Staffords, who found a lot of enemy in small pits covered over
with brushwood to escape observation from the air, disposed of
large numbers with the bayonet. The prisoners came from three
different divisions, the 4th Guard and the 19th and 45th Reserve;
and it was elicited from them that the first and last of these had
reinforced the 19th, the normal garrison of the line, for a
counter-attack which the British had anticipated by ten minutes.
The British barrage had therefore descended on an area packed
with troops, and the tremendous casualties it had inflicted had
taken the heart out of the survivors.

20 Brigade advanced for the Blue Line at 8.10 am, and although there
were some difficulties, gained their objective with remarkably few
casualties. Things were not so straightforward for 91 Brigade, due to
the problems that had confronted the 21st Division. This meant that the
Brigade's right flank was uncovered in the advance towards the Blue
Line. 22/Manchesters came under heavy fire from Joiners Rest, but
achieved the Blue Line with help from 21/Manchesters.

Problems had been caused by the fact that the neighbouring
Australians had gone some 150 yards off course to their left, and their
neighbouring 7th Division had followed them. This had a knock-on
effect on 91 Brigade, which also moved leftwards, and yet its weakest
point was on the right, for the 21st Division was held up on its first
objective. 2/Queen's were ordered forward from their reserve position
at Hooge, but lost their CO, Second Lieutenant (temporary Major)
Bernard Driver MC, before they set off. He is buried at Perth (China
Wall) Cemetery.

On arrival at the front line, Lieutenant-Colonel Beaumann (1/South
Staffords) put two companies along Jolting Houses road, facing south
and thereby guarding the right flank, one in Jetty Trench and the other
in the Butte as a reserve. Strong points were constructed by 528 Field
Company RE, two on the right to cover that exposed position, whilst a

JOIST FARM

second line had been dug and made into a good line of defence. Although the Division's new position was not subjected to a counter-attack, life was far from easy, and indeed more casualties followed over the next few days than had bee incurred in the advance.

21st Division's Attack
62 Brigade

3/4 Queen's took over the front held by 8/Leicesters – or most of it, as the 7th Division's front had slipped slightly to the right to incorporate the Jetty Wood section – on the night of 2/3 October. The objectives for its attack were: the Red Line, J.11.c.60.55 to J.11.a.85.30, and secondly the Blue Line, J.11.d.65.75 to J.12.a.1.5, a depth of some 1200 yards. The rest of the Brigade came up on the night of the 3rd, taking up positions on the eastern side of Polygon Wood – positions which were in full view of the enemy in daylight.

The War Diary commented that the 'configuration of the ground and the natural obstacles gave every advantage to the defenders'.

The place of assembly was thirty feet below the first objective and in full view of the enemy. Three streams separated the opposing forces. Each stream ran through soft and boggy ground 50 yards in width. This ground had been churned by continuous shelling to an almost impenetrable morass. Scrub covered the slopes of the small spurs and this was all heavily wired. About 50 yards to the east of the Polygonbeek and again to the east of Jetty Warren concrete blockhouses, some containing three compartments, and each provided with loopholes, and manned by garrisons of 20 or 30 with machine-guns and trench mortars, commanded all approaches. 4 feet to 5 feet deep trenches were sited on all the prominent positions. The beds of the streams were swept by machine-gun fire from Cameron Covert and Polderhoek Chateau. As seen in daylight, after the attack, the position seemed impregnable.

View to the north west from the Reutel Road. It clearly shows the difficult terrain which the 21st Division had to move across during their attack. The valley of the Polygonbeek is to the rear.

POLYGON WOOD

THE HIGHER GROUND OF THE FLANDERS I LINE

The attack was to be led by 3/4 Queen's, with the second objective taken by 12/13 Northumberland Fusiliers on the right and 10/Yorkshire on the left; 1/Lincoln was to be in reserve. However, on the approach march 10/Yorkshire was badly mauled by German shelling in Glencorse Wood and Black Watch Corner.

1/Lincoln took two and a half hours to cover the four miles from Zillebeke Lake to their position, where they arrived at about midnight. Heavy shelling continued over the whole area during the night and the moving troops were silhouetted against the light of the burning ammunition dumps. Under cover of the darkness guiding tapes were put out by the three leading battalions and posts were pushed forward to Polygonbeek so that the enemy would remain unaware of what was taking place.

At 5 am the CO of 1/Lincoln, Lieutenant-Colonel LP Evans, returned from looking at the assembly positions and, acting on alternative Brigade orders, switched his battalion with 10/Yorkshire, as the latter had suffered such heavy casualties. When the German barrage came down it caused few casualties in the Brigade as all the attacking battalions came forward so that their total depth did not exceed two hundred yards.

To the rear of the line the Machine Gun company, described as a 'Barrage Group' had set up its position around J.9.d.9.2, presumably making use of the bunkers (which still exist) and trench line in that vicinity. They were established on 3 October and set about fixing their barrage lines and SOS positions, and brought up the required 100,000 rounds of ammunition – actually brought up by both limbers and mules.

An officer and a lance corporal of one of the Machine Gun companies take bearings to be used by their guns for a barrage line.

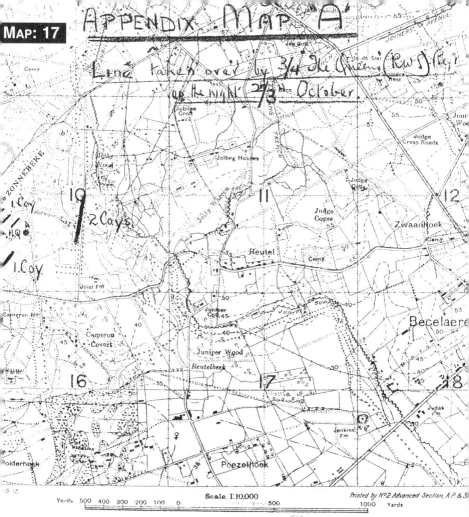

The attack of 62 Brigade. Positions held by 3/4 Queen's on the night of 2/3 October.

At 6 am the attack went forward, but

the immediate obstacle of the Polygonbeek, with its mud and tangled wire was found so difficult to negotiate that the artillery barrage crept away from the advancing troops and was not regained until Jetty Warren was reached.

A few mud mats and trench boards, which had been brought up with great difficulty, and were placed in position, considerably helped the crossing of the troops and more particularly of the lightly equipped leading platoons. [At this stage 10/Yorkshire occupied the vacated front line position.]

Several unexpected and well-hidden concrete emplacements

103

on the eastern bank of the Polygonbeek, each manned by a garrison of 20 to 30 men and three machine-guns, immediately the barrage had passed, opened fire on the advancing troops, causing many casualties.

'A gross case of treachery' took place near Jupiter Trench when a German officer put up his hands to surrender; Lieutenant Cooper went forward to receive it, but the German officer whipped out his revolver and shot him. Cooper has no known grave, and is commemorated on the Tyne Cot memorial. The men who witnessed this promptly riddled the body of the German with bullets. On another occasion an inner compartment of a mebus opened fire after the outer garrison had surrendered so that 'it was necessary to kill all the Germans in the post'.

The offensive sprit of 3/4 Queen's in this, their first, fight was beyond all praise and their recent hard training enabled them instinctively to work around these Mebus and reduce them with skill and rapidity.

A combination of factors had meant that by this stage in the proceedings the covering barrage was 250 yards off. The resistance of a number of these fortifications, German fire from the right and the natural obstacles all held up the prescribed rate of advance. Both Evans and the commander of 12/13 North Fus realised the seriousness of the situation, and closed their battalions still tighter to the Queen's

The OC 1st Lincoln R. passed his two leading companies through the northern companies of the Queen's, scrambled across the bog of Jetty Warren and rushed the first objective, killing large numbers of the enemy. The Northumberland Fusiliers, ably backed up the Queen's and reached Judge Trench at the same time. The trenches, which were found to be in very fair condition, were filled with the troops of the 19th Reserve Division, which Division had just been brought over from the Riga [part of the Russian] *front.*

The bayonet was freely used and large numbers of the fleeing enemy were shot with the rifle. Hand grenades and P [Phosphorous] *bombs cleared the mebus and rifle grenades the more distant shell holes. One mebus was apparently set on fire by a P. bomb and burnt furiously, the whole garrison being shot as they fled or burnt to death before they could emerge.*

12/13 N.Fs had again to take part in a severe fight for a mebus about J.11.c.7.8, large numbers of Germans being killed and a few prisoners taken.

An incident involving 'a small soldier' of 12/13 North Fus was reported with some relish. He met a German soldier running around a mebus.

> *A guttural remark of the German was replied to with 'Nong comprez'; 'From Riga', said the German, 'To hell' said the Englishman, and pushed his bayonet into his opponent's body'.*

A rather bizarre incident involved the chaplain, the Rev Mazzini Tron, who was to collect a DSO for his performance that day whilst serving with the Northumberland Fusiliers.

> *His cheerful demeanour had a great influence in keeping up the spirits of al ranks whilst assembling for an attack. He went forward with the attack and exposed himself fearlessly* [how changes in word usage cause a smile!] *in attending to the wounded, regardless of his own safety. His unceasing efforts under heavy fire and the most adverse conditions are worthy of the highest praise.*

This distinguished cleric was born and brought up in Gateshead, and then went to work in the Bush in Australia before joining the AIF and serving in Gallipoli. On the evacuation of the force and its dispatch to France he transferred to the British army. In the course of his war service he also collected an MC and Bar. It was not only for tending the wounded that he got himself noticed on 4 October. The Brigade War Diary notes,

> *A German officer rushed at the Rev Tron and nearly tore his coat from off his back. The Padre, who is a bit of a boxer, struck the German in the face until they broke apart. Unslinging his glasses, the German thrust them into the hands of the astonished clergyman and tendered his surrender.*

Rev Tron's was definitely the form of Christianity known as 'muscular'. After the war he became the Rector of Rushock in the Diocese of Worcester.

> *The artillery barrage, which had halted 150 yards beyond, now contained a percentage of smoke shells.* [This was done for a variety of reasons; cover for the consolidating troops and those preparing to advance; an indication to the troops that this was the First Objective, and the point at which to pause; and an indicator to various observers, both in the air and on the ground.]
>
> .... *Direction up to now had been fairly well maintained, considering that the Polygonbeek, Juniper Trench, the almost impassable bog called Jetty Warren and Judge Trench all lay at different angles from one another. Despite the fact that the*

situation must have been obscured by dust and smoke, the fire of the enemy's machine-guns from Cameron Covert and Polderhoek Chateau steadily increased in volume and caused great casualties in our ranks. While reorganising Lieutenant-Colonel Dix, commanding 12/13 North Fus was shot [he is buried at Tyne Cot] *as well as his four company commanders. The fire raked our ranks. Each of the three leading battalions had now lost 40% of its effectives and no battalion had more than six officers left. Gaps occurred in our line as a result of the obstacles encountered and the inequalities of the ground.*

The general situation at 6.30 am on October 4th was as follows:- 3/4 Queen's consolidating along the whole of the first objective, less one company digging in its immediate support. On the left, in continuation of Judge Trench, elements 1/S Staffs, on the right the KOYLI of 64 Brigade. In advance on the left 1/Lincoln forming for the attack on the second objective [C and D were in front; A and B reorganised in Judge Trench, though A was moved up shortly before the advance to the second line commenced]. *In the trenches on the right the Northumberland Fusiliers forming up for the same purpose. It appeared that the 5th Division were held up at Polderhoek Chateau, with the result that 64 Brigade was being badly enfiladed by machine-gun fire from this area. This in its turn effected the 12/13th who, when the time came at 8.10 am to advance on the second objective, found their right flank in the air and at the same time were raked by*

German machine gun position engaged in indirect firing. This sort of barrage aimed to harass parts of the enemy line that were regularly used for supply and communication.

*intense machine-gun fire from the Chateau. After advancing 150
yards they dug in.*

*1/Lincoln on the left, slightly protected by the curve of the
spur, and only subjected to indirect fire from the Chateau, some
machine-guns from Judge Copse and the two isolated mebus and
numerous snipers ensconced in shell holes, obtained their final
objective and consolidated. The line was not continuous but was
sound in principle, with no dead ground uncovered. The Brigade
had, owing to the inequalities of the ground, extended its flanks
and had encroached into the 7th Division area. 3/4 Queen's had
thrown back a defensive flank on the right in expectation of a
counter-attack from Reutel. While the attack was proceeding the
enemy heavily shelled Polygon Wood and the back areas.*

Two guns attached from the Machine Gun Company to 12/13 North
Fus lost direction and found themselves in 64 Brigade area, actually in
front of that formation, which was held up. However, fortune played a
hand, because their positions were ideally placed for both defensive
and offensive action, and so they remained put. Two other guns
wandered into the 7th Division area, 'where they did little use'. The
four attached to 3/4 Queen's suffered a mixed fate – one was destroyed,
one was withdrawn back to the spur to increase the volume of fire and
two were used to reinforce the right flank. It is interesting to note that
the gunners had five sappers attached (to assist with the construction
of strong points) and their own medical orderly. The gunners also
suffered from the German defensive barrage on their position in
Polygon Wood, as nearly all the officers were all knocked out. The
machine-gun officer's report has an interesting observation that

*In the case of the carrying parties it was found that a greater
proportion of full NCOs would have rendered these parties much
more efficient.*

This suggests that the carriers were rather too quick to take shelter –
and who can blame them – instead of rushing forward, if such were
possible in the conditions, with their valuable burden.

1/Lincoln set off, but soon suffered the consequences of an 18 pdr
gun firing short – one shell wounded two officers and six men.

*Two hundred yards further, a pill box at J.10.d.5.5. (about
three hundred yards north east of Joist Farm and just in front of
Juniper trench) was encountered: the leading waves passed
without meeting resistance.* [This pill box, or one very close to
its location, still stands.] *A machine-gun opened fire from this
place, inflicting casualties. At this stage Lieutenant-Colonel*

Possible the bunker captured by Lieutenant-Colonel Lewis Evans. This deed, amongst others, won him the Victoria Cross.

Evans, assisted by an officer of the Machine Gun Corps and several men of the Lincolnshire Regiment, advancing from two directions, silenced the machine-gun, reached the pill box and forced the garrison to surrender.

Lewis Pugh Evans was what some social commentating military historians would describe as a typical member of the pre-war officer class. From a wealthy family, he was educated at Eton and Sandhurst and was commissioned into the Black Watch in 1899. He saw service during the Boer War and subsequently in India, and was one of the last class to pass out of the Staff College at Camberley, in August 1914, before that institution closed for the duration. He was typical of many of the much maligned and despised staff. He started his war as a G3 at the War Office ('G' means operational as opposed to Q and A, which relates to administration). However, by the end of September he was serving as an Observer with the RFC before returning to his regiment 1/Black Watch, as a company commander, at the end of December. On 1 May 1915 he became Brigade Major (another staff job) of 7 Brigade in the 3rd Division and won a DSO for his actions at Hooge on 16 June 1915.

When, after troops had become much mixed up, he continually moved up and down the firing line under heavy fire from 10 am until midnight, reorganising units and bringing back their reports.

He then moved to the divisional staff in March 1916, this time as a G2 with 6 Division, before becoming CO of 1/Lincoln in March 1917. For his actions in the attack on 4 October he was to win the VC, which was gazetted on 26 November 1917.

Lieutenant-Colonel Evans took his battalion in perfect order through a terrific enemy barrage, personally formed up all units, and led them to the assault. While a strong machine-gun emplacement was causing casualties and the troops were working round the flank, Lieutenant-Colonel Evans rushed it himself and, by firing his revolver through the loophole, forced the garrison to capitulate. After capturing the first objective he was severely wounded in the shoulder, but refused to be bandaged, and reformed the troops, pointed out all future objectives and again led his battalion forward. Again badly wounded, he nevertheless continued to command until the second objective was won and, after consolidation, collapsed from loss of blood. As there were numerous casualties he refused assistance, and by his own efforts ultimately reached the dressing station. His example of cool bravery stimulated in all ranks the highest valour and determination to win.

Although quite seriously wounded, he was back on the Western Front in early January, and back to his old battalion; but within three weeks he was transferred to the ultimate accolade of a pre-war regular soldier, command of his own first Battalion, 1/Black Watch. He won a bar to his DSO (having already picked up a Croix de Guerre) for his actions at the three day Battle of Givenchy in April 1918.

On the first day he was moving about everywhere in his forward area directing operations, the next day he personally carried out a reconnaissance for a counter-attack, which was carried out on the third day. It was largely due to his untiring energy and method that the enemy were checked and finally driven out of our forward system.

In June 1918 he was appointed commander of 14 Brigade (32nd Division) and was appointed CMG in May 1919 for his services whilst commanding the Brigade during the Hundred Days and the Advance to Victory. This great soldier, whose career was not unremarkable for many staff officers, with the notable exception of the award of a VC, remained in the army for the rest of his professional career, and died in 1962.

The War Diary records that there was no outstanding incident on the Brigade front until 3 pm, when the enemy was seen to be massing behind Cameron Covert preparatory to counter-attacking the 5th Division. There were no effective signal arrangements, apart from pigeons, until about 6 pm; a bird was dispatched and brought down

> *such an accurate and heavy artillery fire on the spot as to disperse the whole force and at the same time causing heavy casualties.*

The CO of 3/4 Queen's noted that the enemy massing at Cameron Covert

> *Seemed entirely oblivious of our presence on the high ground north of Reutel and so fell an easy prey to our guns. Even if our artillery had not shelled this concentration, the commanding position of our companies would have enabled them to cause very severe casualties to the attacking force.*

By this stage 1/Lincoln had been reduced to some four officers and 160 other ranks, having set out with approximately 500 men. During the night both it and 12/13 North Fus were relieved by 6/Leicesters from the reserve brigade, 110, and these battalions then moved out to a reserve position near Zillebeke Lake. During the following night 6/Leicesters moved their posts forward and effectively occupied the ground of what was intended to be the final objective. When 1/Lincoln went out of the line it was found that the battalion had been reduced to only six officers and the losses were recorded as 24 killed, 167 wounded and 36 missing (almost certainly killed) – 227 in all.

The Germans started shelling the new line heavily, at intervals, from about 10 am on 5 October, and this continued until the Brigade was relieved on 8 October by 22 Brigade (7th Division).

> *The operations from October 3rd to October 8th had cost the 62nd Infantry Brigade heavy casualties, 74 officers out of the 86 who had gone into action and 1279 other ranks. Despite their losses, the scarcity of food and water (the carrying of which was almost stopped by the continuous enemy barrage), and the wet, the morale of all ranks remained extremely high. The victory had been a complete one and the enemy signally defeated.*

There is a rather sad footnote to this section. The Brigade Commander was killed on 28 October 1917. Brigadier-General CG Rawling was gazetted for the DSO in the New Year Honours on 1 January 1918; he already was the holder of the CMG and the CIE. He was killed by a shell at the door of the large Hooge Crater dugout, habitually used as a Brigade HQ.

> *He had gone out to supervise personally the unloading of some wagons which had been interrupted by a burst of shell fire.*

Hooge Crater, blown by the British in 1915, had become by the autumn of 1917 a busy headquarters location. It was here that Rawling was killed.

The incident was characteristic of his disregard for danger, which he had shown among other ways by a habit in ordinary trench warfare of walking over the top instead of by communication trenches as was laid down in orders for everyone else.[2]

64 Brigade

This Brigade was commanded by Brigadier-General Hugh Headlam. He was educated at Wellington, a school with a very strong military tradition, situated in the shadow of Sandhurst, to which he moved in 1895. He served on the staff during the Boer War and subsequently in the Sudan. He won a DSO for distinguished conduct in the field on 23 June 1915 whist serving as a major in the York and Lancaster Regiment. He became a Temporary Brigadier-General on 12 June 1916, and was created a CMG in 1918.

On 1 October Brigadier-General Headlam wrote an appreciation of the prospect facing his Brigade, and he makes a number of pertinent points. For example before the British advances of 20 and 26 September the Germans had the relatively safe area east of Passchendaele Ridge in which to assemble their counter-attack troops. Whilst they still held the ridge, and therefore the assembly area, the fact was that it was no longer safe; and, indeed, assuming the advance went well, this forming up area would be under the standing barrage if the second objective was taken. It was also inevitable that German morale would not be good after the two blows of late September, especially as their counter-attacks had almost entirely failed, and in no case made a significant tactical gain. The increased number of voluntary surrenders showed some indication of the state of things.

Headlam then offered an analysis of the ground to be covered.

The objective of the Brigade is the extreme left of the high ground of the German position. From the starting off point, the ground falls till it reaches Polygonbeek. The ground on either side of this is marshy and churned up by shells. The beek is narrow but has water in it. Unless, however, there is heavy rain, the ground is passable at a slow rate. The fact that the Germans have been able to counter-attack across this ground proves this. On the right boundary of the advance, the road which crosses the beek will probably assist matters On the east of the beek the ground rises fairly steeply up to the top of the ridge which is reached on the first objective. The advance to the second objective is on top of the ridge. The chief obstacles to this advance are the village of Reutel and the line of block-houses running northward from the east end of the village.

As this is the left of the German line on the ridge top, we must expect that the defences have been carefully and strongly prepared, and success will, to a great extent, depend upon the assaulting troops keeping right up to the tail of the barrage.

The strong points in the Poezelhoek Valley are likely to be well

Members of a German Eingrief Division rushing to counter-attack.

equipped with machine-guns, which may harass our advance from the right flank. Special artillery arrangements have been made to deal with this matter.

He also discussed the problem of German counter-attacks, the direction from which they were likely to come and the way in which they were to be countered.

The plan for the attack is based on an attack in depth. The narrow front 250 yards) allotted to the Brigade permits of this. One battalion attacks and occupies first objective and a second battalion, assisted by one company of support battalion, attacks and consolidates second objective. Two more companies of the support battalion move up to positions of readiness east of Polygon Beek and the remaining company holds our original front line.

Headlam is keen to underline that commanders on the spot, from platoons upwards, must act on their own initiative and as circumstances dictate – but must also inform superiors up the chain of command as to their actions.

The Brigade began its move up to the front on the night of 2 October, relieving part of 110 Brigade. 9/KOYLI took over the front along the line of the road, from the Reutel-Hooge road on the right to a point some 300 yards west of Joist Farm, therefore holding a front of some 250 yards. 15/DLI was in support, instructed to have two companies west of Glencorse Wood and two east of it, but due to shelling, casualties and lost guides they established themselves in the south east corner.

15/DLI continued to suffer from the searching German artillery fire the following day, so much so that the Commanding Officer, Lieutenant-Colonel Falvey-Betts DSO, felt that his men were so shaken and had suffered so many casualties that they would not be capable of undertaking the attack on the second objective. 10/KOYLI was ordered, therefore, to take the second objective, 1/E Yorks to be in support and 15/DLI in reserve. The Brigade Major was dispatched at 10 pm to tell the Commanding Officers of the battalions coming up from the rear, who were setting off at about this time, about the new arrangements. This caused no great difficulty because the original planning (as for other brigades involved in the action) had allowed for this possibility.

The reserve company of 1/E Yorks got caught in a barrage, and was effectively put out of action, but apart from this the assembly on the line, behind the tapes, went off remarkably well. 9/KOYLI were to

Looking eastwards over the Polygonbeek on the Hooge to Reutel road.

enjoy the benefit of a rum ration issued just before zero. (Interestingly enough the rum ration can still be issued in the army; it was abolished some years ago for their naval counterparts when Lord David Own was Minister of State for the Royal Navy.)

The advance commenced exactly at zero. It was almost immediately subjected to heavy rifle and machine-gun fire which caused casualties. Joist Farm was found to be strongly held and wired in front, and its resistance broke up formations. The farm was eventually taken by mixed parties of 9 and 10/KOYLI, the arrival of a tank in the vicinity apparently helping matters. In the meantime the left had advanced meeting only slight opposition. Just west of the Polygonbeek Germans were met in some force and hand to hand fighting took place. The crossing of the beek was a difficult matter and during its passage the troops were subjected to severe enfilade fire from the direction of Juniper Copse and the right flank generally. A considerable number of men, finding the crossing almost impossible, eased to their right and crossed by the road on the right flank [ie the Reutel-Hooge road] *afterwards used by tanks.*

On the east side of the beek there were several concreted strong points which offered resistance and which were promptly dealt with. One of these pill boxes was a battalion HQ. On arriving at the top of the hill, Juniper Trench was found strongly held but the Germans, except at one or two points, did not offer serious resistance. The first objective was finally reached up to time and close to the barrage.

By this time the attacking troops were very much mixed up. Not only were the 9 and 10/KOYLI there, but there were me of the Queen's and 12/NF (62 Brigade) on the extreme right and a also a platoon of 1/DCLI (95 Brigade, 5th Division) which had lost direction and joined 9/KOYLI.

The results of the original check on the right, the fighting before the first objective was reached, the confusion in the

114

crossing of the Polygonbeek, and the many casualties (especially to officers) incurred in the advance, caused the further advance to the second objective to be a somewhat disorganised and piece meal attempt. The troops did not succeed in reaching their objective but dug in about 100 yards east of the first objective. A tank assisted in this advance and men followed it, but it came back and the men with it, losing direction, did so too.

1/East Yorks were to come forward from their support position with two companies at the start of the advance on the second objective; however, when the officer commanding, Captain Case, saw the exposed right flank, he led his men to cover it. A company of 15/DLI was ordered up to dig in on the Joist Farm Line. Actually this was almost half the battalion, because it had been reorganised into two companies after the hammering it had received on 3 October. The Officer Commanding, Lieutenant Sedgwick, also appreciated that the 5th Division advance had been checked, and so arranged his men facing south east and south along the road on the north side of Cameron Covert, just south of Joist Farm. This defensive flank was established by 2 pm.

A possible counter-attack at 1 pm was halted by the artillery.

Shortly before 2.30 pm it was seen that a serious counter-attack was about to take place. Enemy were massing in numbers variously estimated as up to 1500 to the south east and south. The SOS was again sent up and rifle and Vickers gun fire opened. [Two of these guns were the one's that lost direction from 62 Brigade.] *Notwithstanding the fire the enemy seem to have advanced with great determination. Machine-guns were seen to be carried into Polderhoek Chateau and large numbers of enemy reached Cameron Covert. 15/DLI opened sustained fire on to these with seven Lewis guns and their rifles. The firing was at 500 yards range and the severest casualties were inflicted on the enemy, who got no nearer and were broken up.*

It was far from clear quite what was happening on the right, in 95 Brigade sector (as mentioned above, they were having a torrid time of

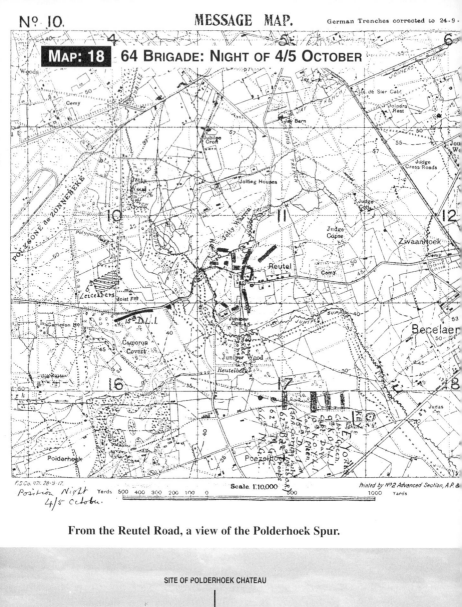

MAP: 18   64 BRIGADE: NIGHT OF 4/5 OCTOBER

Scale 1:10,000

Position Night 4/5 October.

F.S.Co. 171. 26-9-17.   Yards 500 400 300 200 100 0   Printed by Nº2 Advanced Section, A.P. &

From the Reutel Road, a view of the Polderhoek Spur.

SITE OF POLDERHOEK CHATEAU

REUTELBEEK

it). The remainder of 15/DLI and its HQ were ordered up to hold the right flank and try and establish contact with the right; they were in position by 1.30 am on the 5th. At almost the same time 6/Leicesters arrived in the vicinity of Joist Farm. 15/DLI now made contact both with troops east of the Polygonbeek and with 1/DCLI at the west of Cameron Covert.

Early on 5 October Lieutenant-Colonel Beyts organised an attack on a pill box armed with three machine-guns in Cameron Covert. The Germans, seeing the preparations for the attack, surrendered. Throughout the day the position remained the same. There was continuous heavy shelling throughout the 5th by both sides. The Brigade remained in position throughout the 6th October. In the evening 95 Brigade established itself in Cameron Covert and took over the area south of the Reutel road up to the bridge over the Polygonbeek. 15/DLI withdrew that night to Zillebeke Lake and 7/Leicesters took over the captured position and 8/9 Leicesters occupied the Joist Farm area in support. 9 and 10/KOYLI and 1/East Yorks then withdrew to Zillebeke.

During night of 7/8 October 8/9 Leicesters moved to a position across the Polygonbeek WNW of Reutel and at 8 am on 8 October the command of the line moved to the 7th Division. [Brigade HQ had been just to the east of Hooge, a little north of the Menin Road.]

15/DLI went back without their commanding officer, Lieutenant-Colonel Falvey-Beyts [Betts in the register]. He was killed during 5 October, and now lies buried at New Irish Farm Cemetery. He, too, received a DSO in the New Year Honours of 1 January 1918.

It was whilst assisting the attack of 64 Brigade that the Tank Corps was to receive its first VC. Unusually it is a most easy action to follow of the ground, and equally easy to appreciate the magnitude of the

GHELUVELT CHURCH

calculated bravery that lay behind it. Captain Clement Robertson was one of the earliest members of the infant Tank Corps, in its day as Heavy Branch, Machine Gun Corps.

By this stage in Third Ypres, Robertson commanded No 12 Section (ie four tanks) of A (or 1st) Battalion the Tank Corps. They were to be used to assist 64 Brigade in the capture of Reutel. Tanks had at least some chance of being useful in this part of the attack. The Reutel-Hooge road provided a reasonable chance of firm ground, despite its battered state, whilst the Brigade faced real problems from its position as the flank Brigade, the right shoulder of the whole British attack. Although the Germans would be likely fully engaged by the infantry on the left of the road, the Germans in the second line positions to the right, in and around Juniper Wood, would have a clear view of proceedings.

As the condition of the ground was bad, he set out accompanied by Private Allen, who had volunteered to assist, to tape out a route. Working all night, and with very little sleep during the day, this task occupied them from 30th September to 3rrd October. On 1st October Private Allen had been blown up by a shell and severely shaken, but with great determination he stuck to his self-imposed duty.

Part of the problem that Robertson faced was not only the route to be taken by his great, unwieldy and lumbering machines after zero, but also he had to get them up to a start line in the first place. As should be clear from earlier descriptions, the approaches to Polygon Wood were persistently shelled by the German artillery, and so he had to find not only a route that was passable by his machines, but also avoid the German defensive barrage. Whatever the route, the machines had to be brought up in darkness, so that he had to ensure that all could be done in some six hours, thereby allowing a safety margin.

It was not until 9.30 pm on 3rd October that Captain Robertson had plotted a satisfactory route. He returned and, without a break, went forward once more, leading his tanks up on foot. They reached their starting point safely by 3 am on 4th October. Except for a few hours he had then been continuously on his feet since 30th September. He now rested for a couple of hours, and at 6 am he went forward again to guide his tanks into action. He knew there was a great danger of the tanks missing their way, so with great determination he led them on foot.

This takes some thinking about. Even today, amidst the placid rural calm of this part of Belgium, it s quite possible to get an idea of the magnitude of this decision. Stop just to the east of the present Joist Farm (built to the south of the original) and look around you. In particular look to the right and observe the field of fire that the Germans had. Now this was bad enough for the advancing infantry, but this man would have been prominent, walking ahead of iron monsters approaching through the early glimmers of light, even if the smoke, dust and splashed mud of artillery shells obstructed the view to a degree. He chose to put himself in a position that invited death. The reason for it was that the drivers would be quite incapable, with their restricted vision and inadequate light, to follow the shambles that had been the road. Yet its hard core foundations were vital if the tanks were to make progress forward. Almost miraculously, the bridge across the Polygonbeek as it heads southwards towards the Reutelbeek, remained intact, or at least usable. It had become even more important because the marshy state of the ground to the north of the road made it an essential crossing point for the soldiers of 64 Brigade.

Captain Robertson was certain that if the tanks, blundering from one muddy crater to another, failed to see this bridge, the action was lost. Deliberately he made up his mind. He would guide them over the other side of the stream. So, slowly and patiently, he walked on, and his brave assistant accompanied him.

Captain Mitchell's account tends to the lyrical and perhaps is over dramatic, as he goes on to describe Robertson's further actions. Actually it is unclear as to when during the action Robertson was killed. His VC was gazetted on 18 December 1917,

For most conspicuous bravery in leading his Tanks in attack

A good indication of the desolation across which the advancing British troops had to move.

under heavy shell, machine-gun and rifle fire, over ground which had been heavily ploughed by shell fire. Captain Robertson, knowing the risk of the Tanks losing their way, continued to lead them on foot, guiding them carefully and patiently towards their objective, although he must have known that his action would almost inevitably cost him his life. This gallant officer was killed after his objective had been reached, but his skilful leading had already ensured successful action. His utter disregard of danger and devotion to duty afford an example of outstanding valour.

Captain Robertson's body was recovered, and he is buried in Oxford road Cemetery. In the far distance, from the boundary wall, it is possible to see Polygon Wood some miles away, dominant on the ridge. His faithful assistant, Private Allen, who even had the foresight to remove all documentation and maps from Robertson's body, survived the maelstrom and was awarded the DCM.

One of his tanks made it to near Reutel Cemetery; another got further north and engaged Germans in the vicinity of Judge Cottages, whilst another swung towards German positions in Juniper Wood after reaching Reutel crossroads. One tank was damaged soon after zero and took no further significant part in the action.

Brigadier-General HJ Elles said of him

Captain Clement Robertson's achievement was the bravest action throughout the campaign of a member of the Royal Tank Corps .... only to the foolish did he seem to die. To his comrades 'his name liveth for evermore'.

After the war, remains of tanks were scattered around near the Menin Road.

The 7th Division and 110 Brigade Finish the Job.

Captain D Kelly was an Intelligence Officer on 110 Brigade staff, and wrote of his experiences (not always terribly accurately) in a book, *Thirty Nine Months with the Tigers*. On the morning of the attack he was attached to 5th Division HQ as a liaison officer, 110 Brigade having been assigned to them for possible assistance in the event of a breakthrough on their front.

> *I arrived about five in the morning at the Divisional headquarters, a small street of very nice huts just outside the village of Dickebusch. It was a cold dark morning, with drizzling rain and gusts of wind and, as standing on the plank-walk in*

21st Division on the night of the 7/8 October 1917.

N° 10.   MESSAGE MAP.   German Trenches corrected to 24-9-17.

MAP: 19

Scale. 1:10,000

Yards 500 400 300 200 100 0 500 1000 Yards

Printed by N°2 Advanced Section, A.P. & S.S.

front of the huts I watched the sudden illumination of the area by a line of gun-flashes and star shells, and heard the incessant rumbling of the guns, announcing that the attack had begun, somehow felt the uncanny horror of the War even more than one would have nearer the scene.

The damp cold soon drove me into the warm and well-lighted G [operations] office, where I had about an hour in which to contemplate magnificent wall-maps, on which the arrangements for the attack looked astonishingly simple to execute. I think it was of this very attack that I obtained later the complete map of the artillery barrages, showing the successive 'lifts' exactly located on the map at every few minutes for over an hour. It seemed when one studied such a map by a electric light in a dry and well-warmed hut, that such an attack could hardly fail, but if one stepped out into the cold and rainy blackness and thought of heavily laden men – carrying rations, rifle, entrenching tools, bombs, box-respirator – plodding forward round the squelchy edges of the water-logged shell-holes, under a rain of machine-gun bullets and bursting shells, the whole focus seemed to be altered. I was rescued from these gloomy thoughts by a member of the staff, and I was kindly invited to breakfast in the A [administration] mess with the Divisional commander.

The shattered ground provided increasingly great problems for the gunners as the advance progressed.

7/Leicesters moved up to Polygon Wood in the afternoon of 5 October, taking over positions in 'consolidated shell holes' from 6/Leicesters. Here they endured intermittent shelling, which included gas shells. In the evening of 6 October they moved up to the front, relieving elements of 64 Brigade in the line in Reutel, A and C companies in the front and B and D in immediate support. In support of the battalion came one company each from the amalgamated 8/9 Battalion. 6/Leicesters were on the left.

On 9 October, at 4.45 am, the battalion retired some 500 yards to the west to allow the 7th Division through to carry out their limited attack. Brigadier-General Steele, commanding 22 Brigade, was to command this attack, which would be launched whilst the major attack, the next stage in the step by step push, took place to the left and north, and which became known as the Battle of Poelcapelle. Steele brought his headquarters up to the Butte, whose dugouts had been repaired by the Canadian Tunnelling Company.

The attack was to be headed by 2/1 HAC on the right and 2/Royal Warwicks on the left, with their objective the Blue Line of 21st Division for 4 October. Taking this line would give observation down the valley of the Reutel and the Polygonbeek.

By this stage the weather had turned, and the conditions were wet and slippery. Zero was at 5.20 am and within thirty minutes green flares indicated that the line had been taken. But, as was so common on battlefields of the Great War, it took a long time for reliable

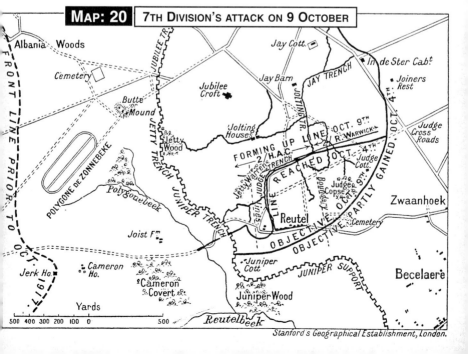

MAP: 20 | **7TH DIVISION'S ATTACK ON 9 OCTOBER**

Stanford's Geographical Establishment, London.

German view from Juniper Cottage.

information to come through.

> Then the HAC reported that they had driven the enemy from Reutel, shooting many down as they made off, and had secured part of the cemetery east of Reutel but were being held up short of Juniper Cottage by heavy fire from machine-guns, and had lost heavily, especially in officers. Next it became clear that there was a gap in the Royal Warwickshires' line near Judge Copse, from which a considerable fire was being maintained. A platoon of the reserve company tried to clear Judge Copse, but without success. A company of 9/Devons was then sent forward, which obtained touch with the left party of the Royal Warwickshires, NE of the Copse; but not till dusk was the position finally made good by another company of 9/Devons, who attacked Judge Copse from the SE and cleared it, thereby completing the capture of the Blue Line.

The HAC history gives a detailed account of the events of the day.

> Before 6 am isolated parties of men had gained their objectives, but communication with Battalion Headquarters was most difficult, and it was not until nearly midday that definite information was obtained to the effect that the HAC had quite early reached their final objective in the village of Reutel, shooting down many Germans as they retreated, and had established posts on the west and south east corners of the cemetery. These posts were reported to have no officers left, except Lieutenant FA Kup, who was lying badly wounded. The left of D Company and the supporting platoon of A Company had considerable fighting in the neighbourhood of the cemetery, one pill box at least being accounted for, and the eight occupants killed. C Company also carried a pill box after a stiff fight, in which most of 12 Platoon were killed. The German garrison were

124

shot down as they withdrew.

At 10.35 am Captain Murray, the Adjutant of the Battalion, went forward to attempt to obtain more accurate information and to clear up the situation, which was then very obscure. Captain Murray made towards the western edge of Reutel and Juniper Cottage, but apparently lost direction, passed unchallenged through a post of a battalion of Leicesters, and advanced beyond the British lines, when he was shot dead by a party of Germans. This gallant officer was observing the enemy's position from a shell hole when he was shot in the chest, but endeavoured to continue his observations and was shot through the head. By midday....no officer of those who took part in the assault remained unwounded.

Captain EFH Murray MC, DCM is commemorated on the Tyne Cot Memorial. He has a DCM, a medal awarded to other ranks; this was not all that unusual in certain regiments of the Territorial London Regiment. These were 'smart'; indeed, such as the HAC and the Inns of Court still are. They might demand subscriptions to enter and remain, payment for uniform – they attracted a certain class. Thus the HAC produced a vast number of commissions, and many of their officers were commissioned from the ranks of the Regiment.

During the day a ration party from the transport lines was caught in a barrage in Polygon Wood and suffered severely, the casualties including many of the drummers.

Tyne Cot Cemetery, which is also the location of the memorial to those who have no known grave and were killed in the later stages of Third Ypres.

Accurate machine-gun fire and sniping from Judge Copse continued to make communication between the Battalion forward report centre and the front line difficult, but soon after midday definite information was received from the Warwicks that a gap existed in their line. This explained the heavy fire brought to bear on the HAC from their left flank. The Warwicks' right was in touch with the HAC in the neighbourhood of the cemetery, and a further attack on Judge Copse was being organised. It was then clear that the front of the HAC had been extended a further two hundred yards to the east.

It appeared later that the first wave of the Warwicks had passed through the copse, capturing a machine-gun and killing the detachment, but the succeeding waves had not succeeded in completing the mopping up of the copse, since hostile machine-gun fire continued from it all day, and it was eventually found that the enemy had five machine-guns as well as some snipers in the copse.

However, the HAC had done their bit; the three attacking companies were reformed as three platoons; 9/Devons completed the business of capturing the Copse on the night of 9 October. The men of the HAC were finally able to pull out, handing over to 13/DLI of the 23rd Division on the night of 10 October, having endured another tough day of shelling and sniping.

That was more or less the end of the story – at least in terms of ground gained. Polygon Wood was firmly in British hands, where it remained until the German spring offensive in 1918; and to which it returned, for good, in the early autumn of 1918.

The HAC lost sixteen officers in the attack. But for the moment I would like to concentrate on a soldier, whose story is sad and poignant, but also is one amongst, presumably almost countless, others.

Donovan, Pte Richard John, 10494, 2nd Bn Hon Artillery Company. 7th Oct., 1917. Age 34. Husband of Evelyn Donovan, of 6, Park Terrace Waterloo Park, Waterloo, Liverpool.

Thus the entry in the Tyne Cot Memorial register. Richard Donovan was a pupil at Ratcliffe College, Leicestershire, a Roman Catholic boarding school. In his last year at school he played in both the 1st XI Football and Cricket teams. His school obituary says of him,

126

His face, with its honest clear eyes, is one that stands out vividly from the multitude of faces that crowd in upon memories of the past, and where the lineaments of others grow dim as the years recede, his is not to be forgotten for its transparent goodness. His character was such as one associates with the ideal schoolboy, keen sportsman, straight-forward and to be relied upon, not wholly innocent of scrapes, unaffectedly good. 'He was of a type,' writes one who was at school with him, 'which it would be difficult to beat – quiet and kindhearted, but full of spirit and grit, the sort of fellow one liked to have in a football team for a tight corner and the clean sportsmanlike way he played games was the clue to the rest of his life.

Of course this is the language that our rather cynical age smiles knowingly at, but it reflects different values, different mores. He was sent to Ratcliffe at short notice, as his father, Cornelius Donovan, died of typhoid fever when Richard was eight years old, and he went with two brothers, William and Frank. Tragedy struck again when their mother also died of typhoid, in their first term, and the children were brought up by a Maiden aunt, Theresa Donovan.

Richard Donovan went overseas on 15 May 1917, doubtless as a member of one of the drafts sent out to bring the battalion up to strength after the losses it had suffered at Bullecourt, when it was reduced to some 250 men. He was killed on 7 October, either in Polygon Wood, 'one shell fell on the track between C and D Companies, killing and wounding half a dozen men' or when it 'came under a heavy barrage on the way to Jolting Houses Trench and sustained further casualties'.

Thus Richard Donovan's family faced his fate, of being raised without a father. His 27 year-old wife was in despair; but his two sons (the youngest of whom was only five months and who wrote to me, 'I saw him only once so I have no recollection of him') also went on to be educated at Ratcliffe.

The role of the Leicesters for most of this time had been one of holding

the line. 7/Leicesters for example, holding the, line, simply notes in the War Diary that they withdrew back to allow the attacking battalions through and then at about 10 am re-occupied their old positions, suffering some casualties as they did so. In the night they sent out patrols to locate 2/1 HAC, 'only a few were found and there were many wounded about. They held no definite line'. The 10th was quiet and at about 5 pm the Battalion began to withdraw. They suffered quite severe casualties whilst coming out o the line, and the last section did not get into Anzac Camp, Dickebusch, until 9 am on the 11th.

In these circumstances it is interesting to look at those engaged in support.

My grandfather, Arthur Cave, the RQMS of 7/Leicesters kept a very sketchy diary. On 4 October he noted,

> *Battalion went back to support an attack at 8.30 am this morning* [having only got in at 3 am the previous morning]. *Foulest place we have struck. Rain, rain, rain and mud.*

Of 9 October he wrote,

> *Started out with rations this afternoon and got back at 10 am the next morning. Immediately had to start out getting rations ready for that day.*

Of all his entries this is one that has made me think considerably: presumably he spent something between eighteen and sixteen hours getting the rations up to the front – one can only hazard a guess at the sights, sounds and physical difficulties of such an exercise.

Kelly comments on some of the problems he faced as a Brigade Staff Officer. He talks of the captured villages of Reutel and Molenaarelsthoek, 'which it would be quite inadequate to describe as being merely blown to pieces.

> *I remember going out with two of the battalion commanders in a joint endeavour to identify Reutel which had figured in a Divisional order as some kind of boundary mark, and that we could not agree as to the precise location! It was purely an exercise in map-reading, as not even one speck of brick-dust – let alone half a brick – had survived.*

> *An equally good illustration of the difficulties of this destroyed terrain was the case of the 7th Battalion*

128

Headquarters. A guide provided by the Brigade we relieved , in order to take the Brigade Major and myself to this headquarters, having wisely disappeared, we spent several hours looking for it, as the map reference was about a thousand yards out, and as, owing to the whole area being under view from Polderhoek Chateau, there was no sign of life anywhere. We knew it was in one of the half sunken pill boxes scattered among the shell holes between Polygon Wood and the Menin Road, but there were dozens of these all under view. In the end we had to give it up and wait until a carrier-pigeon reached our dugouts with the exact map location.

DA Bacon, at 9/Leicesters Headquarters, gives a vivid description of what it was like to be in this support area, which it needs to be remembered was often more heavily shelled than the indeterminate front line. On 6 October the 8/9 Leicesters moved up to the line, with headquarters for the battalion to be established in the rear of Cameron Covert [in fact it appears they were just to the east of Polygo Wood, north of the Reutel Road].

Rain fell heavily at 10 pm, and after wandering about for an hour, stumbling over barbed wire and into trenches in the darkness, and being shelled the while, the site was at last found. The position was not enviable; a small and narrow network of trenches, shallow and barely formed, just outside the eastern edge of Polygon Wood, provided such cover as was available. For the remainder of the night a miserable time was spent – all were drenched – and there was afforded little cover from the heavy enemy fire, both artillery and machine-gun. As well as could be

This photograph graphically illustrates the enormous logistical problem of carring everything up the line.

managed with the few tools at our disposal, the trenches were deepened and made defendable. The ground round about this little stronghold was strewn with dead, chiefly enemy, the result of the fighting on the 4th. As dawn broke, our artillery opened a concentrated defensive barrage, to which the enemy replied vigorously.

Throughout the next day great activity reigned. Hostile aircraft were particularly active, dropping many bombs and emptying machine-gun drums into our lines. There were no changes of disposition in the morning or the afternoon, though a heavy artillery duel was in progress – the shells from the enemy chiefly consisting of 5.9", 8" and high velocity missiles. About 4 pm the violence of the enemy fire increased and after 30 minutes became intense. Quickly a British SOS was seen to go up on the right and, as a precaution, the 9th Battalion [the composite battalion was split in two – the 9th part, with two companies, was in the front of Polygon Wood, the 8th part, also with two companies, was at the rear of the wood] *assumed battle positions, a hostile attack being apparently imminent.*

This highly tense atmosphere remained through the night, and it was that evening when the Battalion was transferred to the command of 22 Brigade. Battalion HQ was moved west into a row of three mebus within the wood in the early hours of 8 October.

These mebusses were all in a derelict condition within, being some six inches deep in water, and the entrances, partly demolished, faced the enemy, thus rendering them exceedingly vulnerable. The only alternative was to wallow in the mud and, despite disadvantages, the former were preferred. Two days were spent in the new positions, no changes in disposition of any kind occurring, but the time was most unpleasantly passed and the conditions were most demoralising for the troops. A fresh artillery duel opened up on the 8th, and continued with unabated fury until the afternoon of the 10th – at times more violent than at others. The weight of it appeared to be concentrated about Battalion HQ especially, though the forward area and indeed the Support Position as far back as Black Watch Corner and Clapham Junction received plenty of attention. The enemy on this occasion made use of very large calibre shells, presumably ranging on the mebusses in the hope of breaking them in and so destroying the only available cover. Around our own particular fragment the fire was directed with deadly accuracy, and a continual downpour of 8 inch missiles, containing high explosive, burst on the roof and landed all round, sending up clouds of mud and splinters. It was absolutely unsafe to go out, and constituted a death trap within; the gap serving as the door was six feet wide and it required but one shell to enter to annihilate the occupants. Like rats in a trap, for two days and nights, we crouched in the waterlogged hovel, and it was again miraculous that, while the roof and walls were hit 40 or 50 times, no shell came in via the opening. On coming into the Line for this tour each man brought up two days' rations with him; further supplies were therefore sent up from the Transport Lines on the evening of the second day. They were brought up by mules as far as Clapham Junction and thence should have been conveyed by the ration party; on the arrival of the party at the junction, however, the enemy was shelling very heavily and the

Fighting conditions meant that sleep was grabbed whenever – and wherever – possible.

party was ordered to dump rations and return. Early the following morning parties were sent down by the companies and one party from Battalion HQ, locations being given them. Between the mud and the shelling the men had a very rough time of it, and for some reason or other could find only a few bags of rations when they arrived at the dump. A number of men were killed or wounded going to the dump and further casualties were sustained on the way back; very few rations arrived for the troops. Two men of the HQ party returned with one bag each, but the second to enter the mebus was hit in the back with a shell splinter on entering, and fell forward, dead; thus they were killed bringing food to others. Such instances were common enough throughout the War, especially in the Ypres area, but few cases ever came to light – one never, or rarely, knew what 'Killed in Action' covered. To say that one became callous would hardly be correct, but it was not a time for sentiment, and during a lull in the shelling the poor fellow was put underneath with all possible speed. Very few more rations arrived during this tour of duty, and this further tended to reduce the morale of the men; cigarettes and tobacco became a minus quantity after the first 2 or 3 days, and the distress of the more ardent smokers became more acute.

It is interesting to note that nowhere in this account of these days does Bacon make any comment on the military activities to the front – perhaps as good an indication as any other of how life at this stage was one of survival in horrible conditions and concern for the next meal and cigarette.

Kelly tells the story from his perspective.

During the next few days my time was spent either loafing in a corner of our stinking dugout at Hooge crater or visiting our depressing line. The latter had become quiet enough in itself, but the routes to it were very frequently shelled. There were two routes, one south of Polygon Wood, past an old pill box, called Black Watch Corner, the other north of the wood and known as Jargon Track. This latter led through a deep hollow, always full of gas, from which nothing was visible but sky and shell holes, and through a group of badly smashed pill boxes – broken blocks of masonry with the steel rods sticking through the gaps – which

An original trench board displayed in the old Cloth Hall museum.

*enjoyed the sinister name of 'Dead Mule Dugouts'. The name
was due to the presence of at least a dozen dead mules lying in
heaps at the side of the track. There were a number of dead men
as well. From this gloomy spot nothing but shell holes could be
seen, and the curious stale smell of gas, putrefaction and thrice
disembowelled earth was overwhelming. One Battalion HQ, I
think the 8th, were in a dugout under the Butte de Polgone [sic],
a mound in the wood, and no mariner ever felt more relief on
getting into port during a storm than one felt on one or two
occasions in approaching that haven of refuge.*

110 Brigade came out of the line for a few days rest, but were soon
back again, until finally relieved in November, to be replaced by the
New Zealand Division.

One of the areas not covered in this guide is that of the artillery; the
7th Division history comments on the horrendous casualties its
gunners suffered. Kelly noted

*A remarkable feature of this period was the system of Army
Barrages. Partly to deceive the enemy as the precise time of our
weekly attacks, partly to anticipate and break-up possible*

counter-attacks, the entire artillery on the Flanders Army front made a habit of firing massed barrages twice a day, usually before dawn and about twilight, for about forty minutes. In addition to these practice concentrations, the artillery were expected to fire rapidly for about twenty five minutes whenever an SOS signal went up from the line, a frequent occurrence owing to the fraying nerves of the men in the line. In this way the average field gun was supossed to fire about a thousand rounds a day, and as it took one horse or mule to carry up every six rounds, and the horse lines had to be many miles back, the strain on transport can be guessed. I have spoken already of the pathetic spectacle offered by the long strings of these bedraggled animals plodding along the greasy shell-swept tracks. But in point of fact the volume of fire was greatly diminished by the enormous casualties amongst the gunners, which made it a sheer impossibility to serve many of the guns. ...In addition, the ammunition dumps were constantly set on fire by the ubiquitous enemy shell-fire, and not infrequently the whole area was illuminated at night by the lurid glare of burning dumps.

Third Ypres had come to an end on this part of the Salient. After 9 October there were several battles over to the north, involving the Canadian Corps on the Second Army Front, which in a number of carefully staged phases finally captured Passchendaele, though rather more importantly the high ground on which it stood. Beyond them Fifth Army also plodded on. The result was a tenable part of the line for the winter months, and a platform, perhaps on which to launch a spring offensive; but it was to be the Germans that launched the attack in a final, desperate fling to defeat the allies, and which came close – very close – to taking Ypres. But in the end it failed, and it was British and Belgian arms that swept over the ridge towards Mons, where it all started for the BEF and where it was to finish.

1. CT Atkinson, *The Seventh Division 1914-1918,* John Murray, London, 1927. This is the basic source for the information on this Division in the guide.

2. DV Kelly MC, *Thirty Nine Months with the Tigers,* p. 85

3. Frank Mitchell MC, *Tank Warfare: The Story of the Tanks in the Great War,* Spa Books with Tom Donovan Publishing, 1987, pp 120 –123.

4. As quoted in Anon, *Fighting Tanks,* Seeley, Service & Co, London, 1929 p. 66

5. ed. G Goold Walker DSO MC FRHistS, *The Honourable Artillery Company in the Great War 1914-1919,* Seeley, Service & Co., 1930, pp. 321 - 326

6. *The Ratcliffian* Vol XI p. 510. Documentation from The Provincial Archive of the English and Welsh Province of the Institute of Charity, The Great War, Box 2.

Chapter Four

THE TOURS

This area of Belgium can get very crowded in the late spring and summer months, especially at the weekends, as people come out for a day or an afternoon away from the town. **Therefore, at this warm time of year, I would recommend that you avoid the weekends.** The woods round about (eg Glencorse, Nonne Boschen, Juniper) are gradually filling with weekend chalet-type housing, and there is a new housing development being built to the south west of Glencorse Wood. The winter months are the best time to come – the high growing crops

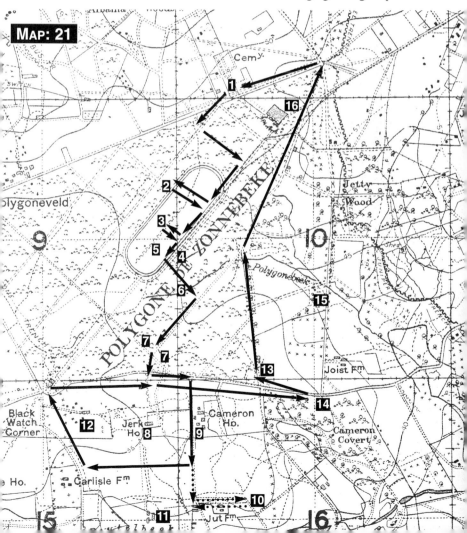

will all be harvested, and not so many people venture out here then.

Only one of these tours has to be done on foot; the others can be done by car, but for the most part it is preferable to do them on foot. The obvious exception is the round circuit to Dickebusch (Dikkebus on modern maps), which has to be done by car or bike.

1. Polygon Wood Cemetery – Polygon Wood - Black Watch Corner – (Jerk House) – Jut Farm – Polygonbeek – Buttes New British Cemetery.

*This tour **has to be done on foot**. It can be very muddy, so walking boots should be worn. The total distance is about 5 kilometres. There is quite a bit to see, so it would be sensible to allow two and a half hours; obviously it can be done in a far shorter time.*

Park the car by Polygon Wood Cemetery (**1**). Please ensure that it is locked and valuables put in the boot – I have had no experience of theft here, but it is an isolated spot and it is better to be safe.

Walk to the west a short distance. Look to your right, over some of the ground that was fought over by the left brigade of the 5th (Australian) Division. Note how the ground begins to slope away to the north. On the modern Belgian maps the contour lines are very close together – but here the interval between them is only two and a half metres.

Enter the wood by the first large, obvious, ride, barred to vehicles by a wooden pole across the track. Proceed down this track until there is a good, clear path to your left, leading you south eastwards and should bring you to the rear of the Buttes Cemetery. You will now find the biggest ride in the wood on your right. Proceed along here for about a hundred and fifty yards and there will be found a much narrower track through the woods. Proceed along this for a couple of hundred yards and you should find a small bunker (**2**) just by the track; there is

another one no great distance to the south of it. These two bunkers are British and were constructed by the New Zealand Division, which held the line here over the winter of 1917 and into the spring of 1918.

Returning to the main track, in due course on your right you will find a drainage ditch, which in winter can be quite full. On your

One of the NZ bunkers constructed in January 1917. There is another nearby.

left there is a bench, and beyond it a picnic table arrangement. Before the bench, and before the ditch makes a sharp right turn, cross the ditch by the main track and head north west, keeping the ditch in its new direction to your left; after about sixty yards or so, and about twenty or so yards from the ditch, you will find a very large bunker. This was named Scott Post **(3)** by the Australians after the CO of the 56th Battalion, which captured the bunker. Scott was killed after the rest of the Battalion had withdrawn, showing his successor around the line. The bunker has two chambers and it is possible to enter it from the rear, though for most of the time its floor is covered with water. It is high – some ten feet or so; and examination will show the scars of battle and the damage done to it by shell fire, exposing a number of the reinforcing rods. The bunker seems to have been part of a trench system that ran along much of the length of the northerly part of the race course.

The entrance to Scott Post; below the interior of one of the chambers under several inches of water.

Return to the main track (this can be 'fun' at any time of the year, but should be especially tricky once the undergrowth has started sprouting). Continue along it until a track is seen to come from the left, after the picnic table is past. Before this track, to the left, will be found another German bunker, **(4)** also captured by the 56th Battalion, and showing considerable signs of damage. This bunker was near the end (within about a hundred yards or so) of the light railway that ran along the southern part of the

This bunker stood adjacent to the light railway line which ran alongside the southern side of the racecourse.

racecourse and back to the rear of Broodseinde Ridge.

Before following this new track take the time to crouch down **(5)** on the main ride and look back towards the cemetery; certainly in winter it is possible to see the 5th (Australian) Division's memorial on the butte (or mound), which gives some idea of the sort of view that German observers would have had from a specially created observation post within it.

Turn along this new track and the wood soon opens out into a large clearing. Quite soon you will cross over the Polygonbeek, **(6)** whose source is off in the woodland to your right. At the next main track crossing turn right, and follow this almost to the edge of the wood on its southern side. Just before the wood emerges – perhaps some fifty

or so yards within the boundary - will be found the remnants of two German bunkers. **(7)** The one on the right has lost all its roof cover; the one on the left is rather more complete, and can be difficult to find in the undergrowth. Both these bunkers caused some problems in the initial attack on 26 September, but were cleared in due course. It was in trenches around here that men of the Machine Gun Company were positioned to provide a barrage for the attack on 4 October.

Continue out of the wood on this track. Almost directly south, some hundred and fifty yards into the field, is the site of Jerk House **(8)**

The 5th (Australian) Divisional Memorial on top of the Butte.

The pair of the German bunker (see page 56) on the southern side of Polygon Wood.

(sometimes called Jerk Farm), a German outpost that was important in much of the fighting on 25 and 26 September. It was in the ground slightly to the west of Jerk House, and a little closer to the road, that the Germans had a number of bunkers that proved troublesome (see the problems of the 31st Battalion) and it was in this vicinity that Bugden carried out the actions that was to bring him the VC.

Proceed eastwards along the road for a couple of hundred yards until a turning is seen to the right; in the wood, nearby, there is the beginning of another ride. Proceed down the metalled road, away from the wood. There is a large complex on your right which coves the ground over which there was heavy fighting on 25 and 26 September and 1 October and, indeed, on 4 October. The wooded area on the left was not there in 1917 or 1914, for that matter), but there was a straggly orchard. A building on the left occupies the approximate site of Cameron House, which forms such a key role for so much of the fighting in September and October 1917. **(9)**

When the road bears right (which it did not do in 1917), carry straight on. The track bears around to the left, and about fifty yards along this is the site of Jut Farm. If you proceed along this track to the end (and beware assorted demented dogs!), at the end of the track **(10)** it is possible to get a good view to the east, across the site of Cameron Covert (or Copse), now gone, and the lie of the land across the Polygonbeek to the north east and east, and towards Reutel.

Return to where the track bore left and turn left, past a pile of assorted rubbish, and a track will be found that leads down towards the Reutelbeek. This gives excellent views across to the hill upon which stood Polderhoek Chateau (which stood, more or less, in a line between you and the new industrial units being constructed on the far side of the valley). Follow the track down and notice in the field on your right

View from near the site of Jut Farm.

Left a closeup of the bunker, below: its open end faces out towards Polderhoek Chateau.

a very fine bunker standing sentinel on the ground rising from the stream. Note that the bunker **(11)** is on private ground and that, should you get permission to view it, the ground round about it is very boggy.

At the bottom of the track it is possible to get excellent views along the valley floor to the east, towards Juniper Wood; the church tower of Becelaere is also quite visible. Returning to the top of the slope, note also the church tower at Gheluvelt to the south. This was in German hands throughout the battle. This knoll of ground, sticking out south eastwards towards the German line, and the cover that the fall in it and Cameron Covert's remnants provided, was a favourite (and natural) approach route for German reinforcements and counter-attack troops. It is quite easy to appreciate here the problem that faced the successive British divisions on this flank of the battle as they struggled to provide a defensive flank when exposed to German fire from Polderhoek chateau and the relatively safe approach route that was provided for German infantry.

Return to the road and turn left. None of the housing that you see alongside the route existed in 1917. Carlisle Farm (see the events of 25 and 26 September) was on the far side of the motorway, just at the head of the north side of the Reutel valley. Continue along the road, looking east **(12)** and contemplating the torrid time a whole variety of British, Australian and German units had here in the last days of September and the early days of October. The road joins the junction with the Hooge-Reutel road and the western perimeter road around Polygon Wood at the approximate site of the strongpoint at Black Watch Corner. Once matters had been resolved on 20 September, the ground west of here, in Nonne Boschen and Glencorse Woods, FitzClarence Farm and across to the Menin Road and northwards to Bellewaarde Ridge, came under persistent and heavy German shelling. During the confusing time of 25 and 26 September, although there was some of the heaviest fighting on the ground, the area to your right (ie east) was left largely alone from the artillery fire of both sides, as the situation and the relevant front lines of both sides was so obscure.

Turn eastwards along the Hooge-Reutel road and follow it along the southern edge of Polygon Wood. Where the track along the eastern

GHELUVELT CHURCH

SITE OF JERK HOUSE

Area where some of the confused fighting on the boundary of the 5th (Australian) and 33rd Divisions' took place on 26 September 1917.

edge of Polygon Wood meets the road is an approximate location for Colonel Bent's **(13)** heroic charge that won him the VC. Continue along the road for some fifty yards or so, beyond the (new) farm buildings. All this ground to the right was occupied by Cameron Covert, **(14)** and the tactical advantage to the Germans of the ground dropping down into the Reutel valley becomes quite clear. Further down the road, now adjacent to it, is Joist Farm; whereas in 1917 it was a hundred or so yards further north and slightly further east.

Return to the track along the eastern side of Polygon Wood and follow it. The main German line on 4 October was off to the right, about three hundred to four hundred yards away at the southern extremity. As you walk further north, and in particular where you cross over the Polygonbeek, the line was captured on 26 September. At this point, about two hundred yards to the south east, **(15)** near the stream, was the site of Captain Fischer's Headquarters, a German commander who courageously tried to hold his line. The German main trench here was known as Juniper Trench. It was also in this vicinity, a little into the wood, that Corporal DA Bacon and the other men of 8/9 Leicesters HQ had such a torrid time in their bunkers when the 7th Division finally took the objectives of 4 October on the 9/10 of that month.

Climbing the slope above the beek look to your right; about two hundred and fifty yards away is the site of Jetty Wood, now gone, although another wood has grown up to the south east of it. Coming to the north east edge of the wood a road (coming from Broodseinde Ridge) may be **(16)** seen coming from the north east. Alongside it there ran a light railway, which then went into Polygon Wood and ran alongside the race track. Go up this road a very short distance – only a matter of a few yards and then look just east of south – there was a major German trench here which became Jetty Trench about two hundred yards further south.

Return to the track, which now becomes a metalled road, and in due course turn left and return to the car. This would be a good time to go and visit the two cemeteries and the memorials that lie close at hand.

Walk/Car Tours

2. Polygon Wood – Anzac – Garter Point – Zonnebeke (Museum) – Molenaarelsthoek – Jolting Houses – (optional Judge Cross Roads) – Reutel – Juniper Cottage and Wood – Jetty Warren – Polygonbeek Bridge – Polygon Wood.

    This is a long walk, and can be covered almost in its entirety by car, though it will require some reversing. The roads are reasonably quiet,

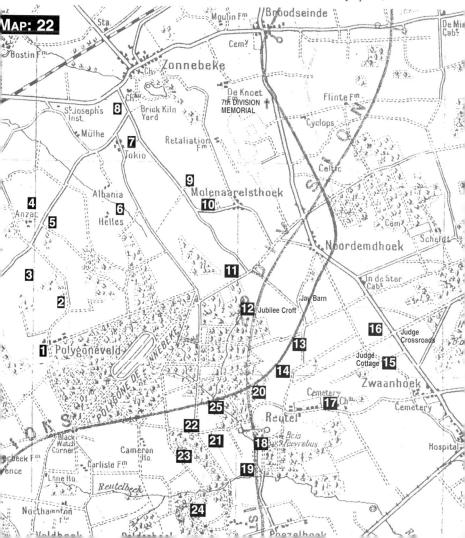

but they are narrow, and it is important that walkers are well aware of the traffic, whilst motorists need to have a clear eye for the rear view mirror should they decide to stop – and get well off the road if they decide to explore on foot.

It is an important walk, as it covers the attacks of 4 and 9/10 October in particular, and also gives considerable insights into the German positions. Even if the Judge Cross Roads section is not covered by foot, it should be done by car, showing the significance of the Broodseinde Ridge to both sides.

The start point for the walk is the car park (1) *on the north western edge of Polygon Wood. This area can be quite busy with traffic, so special care should be taken in both entering and leaving the car park.*

The distance covered is about eight miles. It involves easy walking, with a couple of sections rather muddy, so good walking boots are again recommended. In Reutel and vicinity there are a number of bars and eateries, so the tour can be halted for refreshments. In the season the area can be quite crowded with people on holiday, slightly mind boggling though this might seem! If the Judge Cross Roads section is covered, add another two and a half miles.

The first part of this walk is largely outside that covered by the book, but it gives some indication of the problems facing the Australian divisions in the attack on 20 and 26 September and enables Polygon Wood to be seen from a reasonable distance away, thereby putting it within the context of the bigger battle.

From the car park come out on to the road and turn left and continue straight on, ignoring the perimeter road of the wood which goes off to your right, to the east. On your left there will be found a restaurant/tea house, and there are a couple of others along the boundary road.

Note how the ground soon begins to drop down; off to your left there are good views across the motorway towards Bellewaarde Ridge (where the 6th Machine Gun Company had their guns sited [near the PPCLI Memorial] to provide the covering barrage for 20 September's attack), Nonne Boschen and Glencorse Wood and well over to the more northerly parts of the battlefield.

See map page 41

The farmhouse to the left of the road is near the site of Albert Redoubt, (2) whilst the wood to the north east is Albania Woods, occupying a rather smaller area today than then. The Wihelm Line (also known as the Veldhoek Line) ran just in front of the Albert Redoubt. The road begins to climb again, crossing various German

144

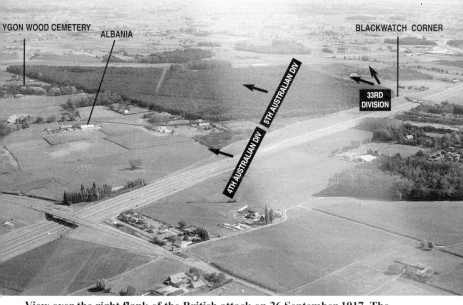

YGON WOOD CEMETERY ALBANIA BLACKWATCH CORNER
4TH AUSTRALIAN DIV 5TH AUSTRALIAN DIV 33RD DIVISION

View over the right flank of the British attack on 26 September 1917. The auto route has carved out the approach route via Nonne Boschen and Glencorse Woods (now grown into one).

switch lines such as Jeremy Switch and Jemu Switch. About a hundred yards short of the junction with the Zonnebeke road look to the left; about fifty yards into the field, amidst the various modern buildings, was Iron Cross Redoubt. **(3)** At the cross roads go straight across; after about a hundred yards look to your right; the farm is on the site of the large observation post known as Anzac, **(4)** the importance of which is discussed at some length in the body of the text. Take this opportunity to look at the views available to the artillery observers, who would have been in the upper room of the two floored bunker.

Return to the cross roads and turn left, towards Zonnebeke. On your left, after some yards, will be seen the drive to the farm on the site of Anzac, and about a hundred yards further on towards Zonnebeke was Garter Point, **(5)** on the right hand side of the road. Not officially part of the objective on 20 September, nevertheless it was occupied. Continue, looking to the right periodically; Polygon Wood stands proud on its high point; Albania Woods may be seen, and before that,

Broodseinde Ridge, seen on the left in the distance, was one of the final objectives in the Third Battle of Ypres. The ridge is here seen from the rather primitive looking Helles strong-point. The 14th Battalion lies under cover of two captured shelters.

on the slope of the ridge along which you are **(6)** walking, may be seen the site of Helles, another important battlefield reference point. This is all ground covered by the attack of 26 September, the ground over which you are looking being the responsibility of the 4th (Australian) Division.

Soon after reaching the outskirts of Zonnebeke a cluster of Commonwealth War Graves Commission signs will be seen indicating, to your right, the road to the cemeteries and memorials in the Polygon Wood area. Do not go down this road, which drops quite sharply, at the bottom of which was a location **(7)** known as Tokio! Carry on to the T-Junction. Should you wish to go into Zonnebeke, do some supermarket shopping, get refreshments or visit the museum, **(8)** turn left. Otherwise, turn right; this was the final objective line for the 4th Australian Division attack on 26 September, but the company commanders decided, sensibly, to push their men some fifty yards further forward to avoid the German defensive barrage that would, inevitably, fall. This action saved many lives.

As you proceed along this road you will be coming over the area where the indomitable Captain Albert Jacka VC made himself invaluable yet again, helping to reorganise and establish order in the left part of the attack. About fifty yards before a road junction, in the ground to your right, was where Captain Henry Wanliss was killed.

A German view towards Polygon Wood from the east north east, a few hundred yards west of Broodseinde Ridge.

POLYGON WOOD

Stop in this vicinity **(9)** to examine the ground to your right, over which the attack had come on 26 September. Then look to your left, where the Broodseinde Ridge may be observed, and the traffic moving on the road that runs along it. The 7th Division Memorial, a cenotaph, is located on this road, and may be seen from here.

It is understandable, standing here, to appreciate the frustration of the historian of the 14th Battalion with the decision not to go beyond the objectives to take the Broodseinde Ridge. Such an action would have been fraught with peril, and already the 18 pounder artillery, with limited range, was having difficulty keeping up with the considerable advances that the British were making. As it was, the German counter-attack infantry were silhouetted as they came over the top of the ridge and their attacks all broke down. Near this spot, off to the east towards Molenaarelsthoek, about two hundred yards along the left fork, was the site of Sergeant Dwyer's VC action. **(10)**

Take the right fork (actually straight on, but the main road bears to the left) and go through the small hamlet of Veldhoek. At the road junction **(11)** stop and take the time to look around and see the tower of Zonnebeke Church rising up from the valley below. Look to your right towards Polygon Wood whilst the Germans still retained control of the ground immediately in front of you.

Here turn left and then almost immediately right. After about a hundred yards there is an unpromising looking turning found between some houses. There was at the time of writing a mail box on one of them. [This track is difficult and not really suitable for cars, so motorists might wish to carry on to the next road junction, turn right and take the next right – the buildings on the corner of this road were known as Jolting Houses. They can pick up the tour from there.]

The farm house on the right, in a state of some decrepitude, was known as Jubilee Croft. **(12)** About three hundred yards away to the south west was Jetty Trench and Wood. The ground drops away quite noticeably towards it, down into the valley formed by the Polygonbeek.

Follow the track to the end: the wood that may be seen to the south west is now a nature reserve and occupies the westernmost part of the feature known as Jetty Warren, which was very boggy at the time of the

The buildings occupying the site of Jolting Houses.

battle. Turn left and notice how good the German field of fire is both to the south and the west. At the end of the road, by the junction, is Jolting Houses, **(13)** which was on the British first objective for 4 October.

On the other side of the road, about a hundred yards or so to the east, ran Jolting Trench, in the vicinity of which Richard Donovan of the HAC was killed on 7 October. A few hundred yards to the north east was Jay Barn, on the site of which there now stands a farm.

Turn right, heading towards Reutel. After a couple of hundred yards, after a double bend in the road, a metalled track may be seen going off on the left in an east north easterly direction. To the right of the double bend, is the easternmost part of Jetty Warren, **(14)** which ran off in a south westerly direction, and was very boggy in 1917. The metalled track soon gives way to a muddy earth track and is impassable to a motor vehicle.

[Extension to the route. Take this track, which follows in the line of the right of the 7th Division attack. Just as it becomes metalled again, look immediately south; the farmhouse below is on the site of Judge Cottage. **(15)** At the junction with the main road (having endured the happy yapping of various dogs) cross over and look at the view to the east – the German rear area where men **(16)** were brought together to launch their counter attacks against the advancing British. Troops here could now see the lush and unbattle-scarred rear areas of the German army – what a contrast to that which they had had to come through! This cross roads (which it was in 1917, no longer so today) was called

View from Juniper Wood in the second line of the German defences. It clearly shows the dominating position of the German defenders.

GHELUVELT CHURCH   POLDERHOEK CHATEAU   REUTELBEEK

Judge Cross Roads. About eight hundred yards to the north west is the site of In de Ster Cabaret, captured by the 7th Division on its left flank. A kilometre to the north is the site of Celtic Wood, where one of the great tragedies of the Australian battles took place in late 1917. This is fully described in *Anatomy of a Raid*, by Tony Spagnoly and Ted Smith, a highly recommended read.

Turn right and head towards Becelaere seeing rather closer up its mighty and impressive church, whose tower is visible some distance away to the west, from the south side of Polygon Wood and beyond. Soon after you come into Becelaere take the turning to the right to Reutel. The ground drops away to your left, and there are excellent views across to the south west, the prominent tower of Gheluvelt church being quite visible. The wood to the west is Juniper Wood, which had caused so much difficulty for the 21st Division.

The road bends slightly to the left and then to the right. Just after this, immediately to the right, on the higher ground, is the site of Reutel cemetery, **(17)** where one of the tanks managed to penetrate on 4 October. At the crossroads at the edge of Reutel turn right; there are plenty of places here to stop for some refreshment should you feel the urge.]

Join the Main Route

Continue past this metalled track into Reutel, and at the cross roads carry on straight ahead. As the road bends to the right, about forty yards or so on, on your right, was Juniper Cottage. **(18)** During the attack of 9 October the situation here was really very confused, and it took some time for the British to clear the situation up to a satisfactory conclusion. On the left is Juniper Wood. Stop by the bus stop, **(19)** soon after the road straightens out to head due south, and look carefully. To the south west, on the high ground, is Polderhoek Chateau, with the modern industrial buildings immediately to the south of it. Notice what an excellent view this gives across to the valley of the Reutel and the high ground beyond, where various British divisions – the 23rd, the 33rd, the 21st and the 5th – all had to endure fire from it. No wonder their task was so difficult. Looking west and slightly north of west, it is also possible to see how well positioned the German defenders were in Juniper Wood and Juniper Cottage to deal with the attacks coming from Polygon Wood and Cameron House, as well as along the valley of the Reutelbeek; and from the north, out of Reutel.

GONBEEK   JOIST FARM   POLYGON WOOD

CAMERON COVERT

Turn around, return to the cross roads at the western edge of Reutel, and take the Hooge road. Note the woodland to your right; about a hundred yards to the north of it is Jetty Warren. **(20)** Juniper Trench crossed the road some hundred yards before it turns quite sharply to the left. After the road makes a sharp turn to the right it soon crosses over a small bridge, **(21)** spanning the tiny width of the Polygonbeek as it makes its way south-eastwards to the Reutelbeek. It was here that Captain Robertson's tank played such an important part in the success of 64 Brigade; and it was somewhere nearby, further east towards Reutel, that he was killed. Soon after crossing the Polygonbeek, stop. To the west may be seen Polygon Wood; just off the road is the modern Joist Farm, **(22)** to the south of its predecessor. Opposite Joist Farm was the approximate midway point of the northern part of Cameron Covert, **(23)** which extended almost to the Reutelbeek to the south and a hundred or so yards further to the east. Look south and see the position of Polderhoek Chateau; **(24)** and south east to place Juniper Wood. Imagine that you were one of those soldiers in 64 Brigade advancing on that morning of 4 October towards Reutel. It feels pretty exposed even today; and bear in mind that Cameron Covert was not cleared until well into proceedings. To your right, and along the road, various units took up defensive positions, including 15/DLI and a number of heavy machine-guns from 62 and 64 and 110 Brigade. Now turn and look to the north and north east. There are a couple of shack-like constructions and a derelict building on the rising valley above the Polygonbeek and quite clear against the green is a considerable bunker. **(25)** This is either the one, or one very close to it, whose capture resulted in Lieutenant-Colonel Evans of 1/Lincoln winning his VC. The difficult nature of the ground shows why progress by the 21st Division was troubled, and, looking south of the road, it is easy to appreciate the problems that the 5th Division had on the same day, exposed as the men were to fire from Polderhoek Chateau and straight up the valley from Juniper Cottage. Continue past Joist Farm and Cameron Covert and along the southern boundary of Polygon Wood. Turn right at Black Watch Corner and then, several hundred yards further on, to your car. The building of the motorway means that it is likely that the site of the various battalion HQs involved in the actions on 25 September and 26 September (including 2/RWF) have disappeared.

It might be sensible to take advantage of the near-by watering holes to recover from your long walk – or nerve-wracking navigation, if travelling by car.

3. Walk/Car Tour. Carlisle Farm – Northampton Farm L Lane and FitzClarence Farm – Glencorse Wood – Verbeek Farm - Lone House.

The start point is in one of the car parks to the north of the Hooge to Reutel road; there is a restaurant/café car park which is most suitable, and has the added bonus of refreshments before and after your walk.

This tour is about two and a half to three miles long. It can be done by foot or by car (or by bike), but foot is preferable, again for reasons of appreciating the ground. There is no off-road walking.

From the car park follow the Reutel road until just before the bridge

On the approach road from Clapham Junction. The new housing on the left is gradually eating away Glencorse Wood.

across the motorway. Take the road that runs parallel to the motorway for some distance. As the road bears round to the right and drops into the Reutelbeek valley, the approximate site of Carlisle Farm (2) will be found on your right. Look across the motorway towards Polygon Wood, Black Watch Corner and the site of Jerk House. It is worth bearing in mind that, whilst the Australians were making progress eastwards out of Polygon Wood, the ground in front of you (and indeed, even in the vicinity of Carlisle Farm) was heavily disputed with the Germans. The vulnerable nature of Elliott's right flank is quite clear to see. On the other hand, it is quite possible to appreciate the problem that faced the Argylls, Middlesex and Scottish Rifles as they tried to deal with a situation of utter chaos in front of them.

Proceed along the road as it goes down towards the Reutelbeek. The buildings on your left are post war; and there is another possibility to get a drink here! It also seems to offer some horse riding, perhaps an alternative way of seeing the battlefield! Past the farm house, take the first turning on the right. Before doing so, look almost directly ahead of you, to the south east, to Gheluvelt Church, and remember that this was in German hands.

Within a few yards, on your right, you will see Northampton Farm, close to one of the old GPO red telephone boxes, the architectural creation of Sir Gilbert Scott. Northampton Farm was one of the many shattered buildings that were used as a Battalion HQ or as an Aid Post.

As you proceed along here bear in mind that all of this area, back to Hooge Crater, was liable to massive doses of German shelling, and was forever being searched by their artillery, seeking to catch ration parties and men bringing up ammunition and mortar shells to the front. There are vivid descriptions in the body of the text of the conditions that the troops faced in this area. At the road junction turn left, towards the Menin Road. After four hundred yards or so a road will be seen coming in from your right, angling back north westwards. Take this road; on the left is the eastern extension of Inverness Copse, and somewhere in there, close to the road, was a German bunker known as the Tower (no longer extant) which featured prominently in the annals of the 23rd Division. On the left, after a few hundred yards, and now in open country, is a building on the site of the chateau. (4) Several hundred yards to the west is Clapham Junction, and an extraordinary construction may also be seen, looking like a cloister without lower walls. This in fact is a rather fancy architectural cover for a water pumping station.

A couple of hundred yards further on, to the right of the road, is the

The Tower; this impressive looking fortification was used by the British after its capture as an HQ.

site of FitzClarence Farm, **(5)** named after Brigadier-General FitzClarence, who was killed in the fighting of First Ypres and whose name appears on the Menin Gate. A little to the south of the Farm was the headquarters of the Scottish Rifles **(6)** when they eventually got up here on the night of 25 September.

At the Hooge Road junction go straight across. After a couple of hundred yards there is a turning to a track on your right; and it was in this vicinity that the Australians dealt vigorously with the Germans who had killed their officer on 20 September. Go a little further down the road to get quite good views to the north and west, the ground over which the British crossed in the latter days of September, forcing the Germans out before them. Return and proceed along the track and almost immediately you will find Captain Brodie's **(7)** memorial. Until recently this stone sat in utter

The memorial to Captain Brodie. Around three sides of it new holiday homes are being built.

TO THE
GLORY OF GOD
AND
IN MEMORY OF
EWEN JAMES BRODIE
CAPTAIN
1ST BATT. QUEEN'S OWN
CAMERON HIGHLANDERS
WHO WAS KILLED AT THE
FIRST BATTLE OF YPRES
11TH NOV. 1914.
BURIED NEAR THIS SPOT.

seclusion, almost unknown. Now it is fated to be surrounded by holiday chalets; but still, maybe more may become curious about the history of this soldier, a casualty of First Ypres. [If in a car, turn around and rejoin the Hooge road; turn left.] [If on foot, it is possible to walk along the track until it meets a metalled road, turn right and come out further east along the Hooge road.]

At the junction with the road turn left, back towards the motorway bridge. On this occasion do not take the Carlisle Farm road but that immediately before it. About three hundred yards down here, on the left, is the site of Lone House (8) (no longer that anymore!). At the end of the fighting on 25 September the British line on the right of the

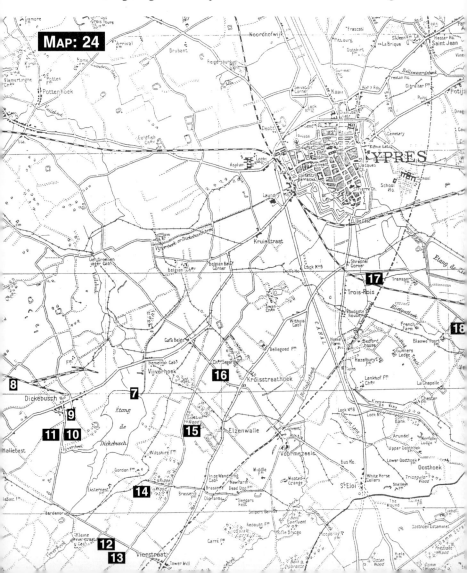

Australians had been forced back to either side of here, with a few parties stuck out in shell holes further to the east.

Return to the road and your car, noting the new Verbeek Farm, **(9)** midway between the road on which lay FitzClarence Farm and that on which Lone House was sited, the large and older building opposite the housing development in the wood.

Car Tour.

4. Hooge Crater – Sanctuary Wood Museum – Ypres – Lille Gate – Dikkebus – Huts Cemetery – Dikkebus cemeteries – Rifle Wood – Scottish Wood – Chateau Segard – Shrapnel Corner – Railway Dugouts – Zillebeke Lake – Perth (China Wall) Cemetery – Hell Fire Corner – Hooge Crater Cemetery and Museum.

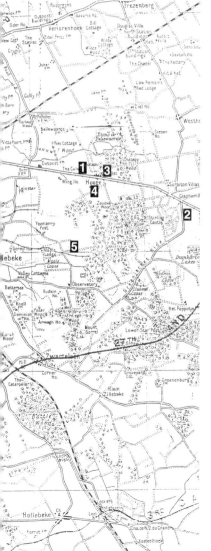

The purpose of this tour is to take the visitor to the back areas and to view some of the cemeteries in the rear areas that are rarely visited but where large numbers of soldiers involved in the operations at Polygon Wood are buried, and where most of them were camped at some stage.

It is quite a pleasurable trip, much of it along country lanes that are quiet and unhurried. The distance to be covered is about eighteen miles, and might make a contrast to a vigorous morning's walking.

The start point is the Hooge Chapel Museum; **(1)** *however, if not already seen, time should be take to look at Clapham Junction,* **(2)** *a mile or so to the*

155

east. Here are the memorials to the 18th Division and the Gloucesters, standing opposite each other on the Menin Road. Near here large numbers of battalions and thousands of men crossed the road on their way to the line in the area of Polygon Wood and to its south.

Depending on the time, it is recommended that you have a snack in the café at Hooge Chapel and take the opportunity to look at the splendid museum housed in the old chapel itself. Before setting off walk up the Menin Road eastwards and get in to a position where you can look into the grounds of Hooge Chateau and can see the huge crater, **(3)** formed by a British mine in 1915 (see this author's *Sanctuary Wood and Hooge*). In fact it is possible to walk around the crater and look at the bunkers situated on its side, but permission should be sought from the hotel. The crater was the site of various brigade headquarters, and it was here that Brigadier-General Rawling was killed on 28 October 1917.

Also take this opportunity to go in and look at Hooge Crater Cemetery, **(4)** standing on the site of a communication trench that ran up from Zouave Wood, which lay to the immediate south west of the cemetery and which no longer exists. Visit Sanctuary Wood Trench Museum if not already done **(5)**.

Drive towards Ypres, noting how clearly the town stands out; the Germans had a splendid view of it from here when they held this part of the line from the summer of 1916 until ejected at the beginning of Third Ypres, only to get back here again in the spring offensive of 1918.

At the roundabout on the site of Hell Fire Corner **(6)** note the British demarcation stone on the road into Ypres; it is immediately on the right as you come off the roundabout. It has a British helmet and equipment on it, and was erected by the Belgian RAC in the immediate post war years to indicate the limit of the German advance and the nationality of the ally which halted them in a particular place. This was done in conjunction with the equivalent French motoring organisation. Proceed towards Ypres, but turn left shortly after a petrol station and by the

Hooge Crater today – compare this with the picture on page 111.

unmissable, tall and ugly water tower seemingly perpetually shrouded by scaffolding. Follow this road round the walls of Ypres and at the Lille Gate roundabout carry straight on.

Take the first major turning left off this road, which is signposted Dikkebus; this will lead through the western outskirts of Ypres and after several kilometres to Dickebusch. Just before this large village there is a turning to the left that would take you down to Dickebusch Lake, **(7)** should you wish to see it. Drive into the village and note the church on your left and the CWGC signs to the various cemeteries. Do not go down there, but remember the location, as you will be returning this way, and the signs are not visible coming from the other direction.

The next turning on the right is signposted on the familiar green and white CWGC sign to Huts Cemetery. **(8)** Drive over the cross roads and at the T Junction (actually it is a minor road off to the right, but there is priority from the right) bear left and keep driving straight on. The cemetery may be seen ahead and to the right, just off the main road.

Immediately to the east of the eastern wall of the cemetery ran a spur from the railway line that came into Ouderdom; it went on to a couple of rail heads in Dickebusch itself. The ground around here would have been filled with camps of various types, horse lines and dumps; whilst close to the line would have been medical facilities, field ambulances and possibly Casualty Clearing Stations. The cemetery has a large number of gunners in it, reflecting the fact that their dead would have been killed in the vicinity and that they could be removed relatively easily to a cemetery. Of the 1100 or so buried here, only six are unknown burials. Amongst those who were brought here was Brigadier-General Rawling; and not far from him lies a son of the Duke of Rutland. They lie amongst hundreds of men from all walks of life from all over the Empire – Australia, New Zealand, Canada, South Africa, the British West Indies and India – as well as six of their enemy on the battlefield. This is quite a contrast to other national cemeteries, where foreigners are not usually found. I think that Captain Albert Ball VC is the only Briton buried in a German cemetery, for example. Equally interesting to note is that I have rarely found a German officer (I have never found one over the rank of major) in one of their cemeteries in France or Belgium. This is because their families could afford to have them repatriated to Germany to be buried there.

The cemetery has good views across to Kemmel, to the south, and Dickebusch and beyond to the east. It is a lovely, quiet spot; almost unimaginable to think of the heaving activity that took place here and in the fields round about all through the summer and autumn of 1917; and in the desperate days of April 1918 when the line lapped up around the edges of Dickebusch.

Return to the village; it was standing on a trenchboard outside a hut nearby that Captain Kelly had his thoughts about what was happening out on the front as he prepared to act as a liaison officer with the 5th Division as the attack commenced on 4 October.

Turn left and then right. Just beyond the church turn left. Opposite the church, and set back from the road, is Dickebusch Old Military Cemetery, **(9)** apparently closed down in March 1915 because of lack of space In fact there is plenty of space, but there were seventy eight French graves taken out after the armistice, which could explain matters. Certainly it came back into use again, because in World War II ten British soldiers were buried here. It is another pleasant spot, immaculate lawns in the shadow of a well-restored church in an unhurried part of Belgium.

Return to the main road and turn left. Almost immediately you will come to Dickebusch New Military Cemetery and Extension, **(10)** **(11)** which between them hold 1100 men. The extension consists of almost 50% Gunners, which is a vivid illustration of how dangerous life in the artillery could be.

Continue along this road until it comes to a T-Junction, with an erstwhile café on the right, on the Hallebast road, needless to say known as Hell Blast Corner (there was another closer to Ypres) to the Tommy. Turn left and after a half mile or so, two cemeteries will be seen off the right hand side of the road.

It is worth stopping to look at both of them, but Kemmel No 1 French Cemetery **(12)** is particularly extraordinary. In 1918 the fighting line reached just to the east of it, and the ground was absolutely pulverised – so much so that this became a 'lost' cemetery, only rediscovered after the war by the French Grave Registration unit. The French burials were removed, probably to the ossuary at Kemmel, to my mind one of the most singularly depressing cemeteries in Belgium, even though the location is impressive. In this British cemetery there are an unusually large number of Germans, buried in a mass grave in row A. These will be casualties from the fighting after the spring of 1918. The vast majority of those buried here are unknown, many of whom were concentrated from the nearby fields. It is a quite unique spot, rarely visited.

At the next cross roads, a couple of hundred yards further on, turn right to go and look at the small Suffolk Cemetery. **(13)** It was started by 2/Suffolk of the 3rd Division in spring 1915. There were only 47 buried here, well over half of them casualties of the spring offensive. It is one of the smallest 'independent' (ie not part of a communal cemetery) CWGC cemeteries in the Ypres area, although not in the ground it occupies.

Return to the cross roads and go straight ahead; after several hundred yards you will be driving along the eastern edge of Ridge Wood; take the turning on the left. The wood is private property, but the scars of fighting remain in it, from the spring of 1918; during the war a light railway ran alongside the northern edge of the road. Beyond the wood Dickebusch Lake may be seen, and on your left, set back from the road, is Ridge Wood Cemetery. **(14)** The cemetery is quite large, with almost 50% of the graves from Canadian units.

Return through the wood and turn left. This area was defended in April 1918, at a key stage in the fight, by the 33rd Division, another connection with the fighting at Polygon Wood.

The next wood, on the right, is Scottish Wood, **(15)** the home of various units of 110 Brigade, and the place from which my grandfather set off to take the rations up the line in the early days of October 1917, involving a round trip of some sixteen to eighteen hours. There were light railways all round this area,

Ridge Wood Cemetery, looking across Dickebusch Lake.

Chateau Segard, the HQ for many formations which fought at Polygon Wood. It was severely damaged in fighting in April 1918.

supplying the various camps and battery areas.

At the next crossroads stop for a moment. Chateau Segard was a few hundred yards into the field to your right front; buildings in the approximate vicinity seem to be rather further to the west than the chateau was. Immediately ahead in the field to the right was Anzac Camp. Turn right and notice the pair of large British bunkers **(16)** in the fields on the left. Alongside the road, on the right, was a light railway. At the road junction turn left, the road to Shrapnel Corner. Descriptions in the text talk of the artillery alongside and activity on this route.

At Shrapnel Corner turn right and almost immediately left, before the railway crossing. The road is pave and not very wide – and quite bumpy – so proceed at a sedate speed. Look to your right and the railway embankment immediately becomes obvious – it was here that various support battalions to the action in the wood were frequently billeted. Zillebeke Lake is to be left; units moving up to the line normally went by way of a track to the north of it which brought them out to the north of the village.

Anzac Camp near Dickebusch.

CHATEAU SEGARD

Wrecked wagons and dead horses were simply pushed to the side of the road.

Pass a large cemetery **(17)** on your right and cross the railway line; take the turning to the left (noticing the 'British' demarcation stone on the traffic island) and go into Zillebeke, crossing the railway line **(18)** and taking the next left, which leads past the church. Drive through the village and on its northern outskirts stop at the large British cemetery on your right, Perth (China Wall). Men going to the front often used the communication trench that ran towards Sanctuary Wood to the north of the cemetery; the China Wall part of the name seems to derive in part from the wall of sandbags that was a feature of the trench. Halfway House was three hundred yards so to the east of the rear of the cemetery, along the track which runs by the south wall of the cemetery. The 'Perth' part of the name seems to date to burials made by 2/Cameronians early in the war.

The cemetery is of particular interest to the contents of this book because a number of British casualties from the Polygon Wood area were concentrated here from German cemeteries after the war; though many of these came from the 1914 fighting. These concentrations are found in an oval arrangement to the right of the cemetery entrance.

Continue on the road to Hell Fire Corner and turn right; note the cemetery at Birr cross roads – some units emerged here en route to the front via the northern circuit of Chateau Wood. It was in this vicinity that log tracks (known as corduroy tracks) and light railways were constructed, pushing forward as the British line advanced.

Return to the café and museum at Hooge Chapel.

Chapter Five

CEMETERIES AND MEMORIALS

The only cemeteries and memorials included in this section are those in the core area covered by the book; others (for example in the rear areas) are included in the body of the text as they are visited. Unusually this section also includes a battle account and tour - the New Zealand Division's attack at Polderhoek Chateau is outside the main theme of the book, but I decided that something had to be said about it, and the context of the New Zealand Memorial seemed to be the most appropriate place for it.

Cemeteries
1. Polygon Wood Cemetery, Zonnebeke
2. Buttes New British Cemetery, Polygon Wood, Zonnebeke
3. Hooge Crater Cemetery, Zillebeke

Memorials
1. The Fifth (Australian) Division Memorial, Polygon Wood
2. The New Zealand Memorial to the Missing, Polygon Wood

1. Polygon Wood Cemetery, Zonnebeke.

The architect of this cemetery obviously took to heart its name when designing the boundary walls. The Cross of Sacrifice acts as a link for the Buttes Cemetery across the road.

The cemetery was started during the British advance in 1917, and was extensively used by the New Zealanders, who were responsible for this part of the front, into 1918. After the withdrawal as a result of the Battle of the Lys it was disused, but was reopened for a short while in September 1918.

It is a battlefield cemetery - that is it was a cemetery that was used during the war and was not expanded after the armistice by the concentration of isolated graves or smaller cemeteries to it. Such casualties were buried in the Buttes Cemetery. Therefore it retains a wartime feel, a sense of urgency about the burials, which are rather scattered, rather than in orderly lines.

To the rear of the cemetery was a large German plot, and it is this cemetery which appears on trench maps of the period. This was called

Polygon Wood Cemetery.

Kriegerfriedhof des Res. Inf. Reg.248 am Polygonenwald, established in 1914 and used in 1915; the 350 or so German graves were removed after the Second World War to one of the two large German concentration cemeteries at Langemark and Menen that are all that remains of their burial grounds in this sector. The gate from the British into the German cemetery was bricked in comparatively recently.

To the left of the cemetery may be seen Albania Woods.

2. Buttes New British Cemetery, Polygon Wood.

The entrance to this cemetery is along a broad walk, dominated by the Butte at its end and hemmed in by the trees of the wood.

This is a concentration cemetery for the scattered burials in the area; there was no concentration of a small cemetery to this place - these tended to be removed to, most notably, Tyne Cot, Hooge Crater and Perth (China Wall) cemeteries. This fact gives this cemetery a special feel. Climb up the stairs to the top of the Butte and look down on the cemetery below. It seems to me that you are looking down on a parade ground; the men, scattered to lonely graves in the lunar landscape created by battle, reformed and restored to their comrades. The graves are almost all from the fighting of 1917, though there are a few from the battle for Ypres in 1914.

There are just over two thousand men, and more than eighty percent of them are unknown. It reflects the fighting in the area, with over a quarter being Australians and there are also a large number of New Zealanders (139), whose presence complements their memorial. Amongst the notable burials are those of Lieutenant-Colonels Scott and Turnbull (see the main text).

The register is often missing for these two cemeteries, due to petty vandalism or (in the case of the register in the cemetery) because the CWGC has got fed up with replacing it. The register includes the details of burials at Maple Copse (not far from Sanctuary Wood) and at Divisional Collecting Post Cemetery Extension, which is to the north east of Ypres, off the St Julian road, so it should be possible to find a copy at these places. An alternative is to inquire at the CWGC office in Ypres.

3. Hooge Crater Cemetery, Zillebeke

The cemetery occupies a relatively narrow frontage on the Menin Road, and then stretches down into the depression to the south. Near to the bottom of the cemetery was Zouave Wood, which was not replanted after the war. The entrance to the cemetery is over the course of the light railway that used to run alongside the Menin Road. As you enter the cemetery the first thing that catches the eye is the circular depression, which is a representation of the crater, now in the hotel grounds on the north side of the road, and further to the east.

The most impressive view of the cemetery is from Canadalaan, the road that leads up to the Canadian Memorial, Sanctuary Wood Cemetery and the Hill 62 Museum.

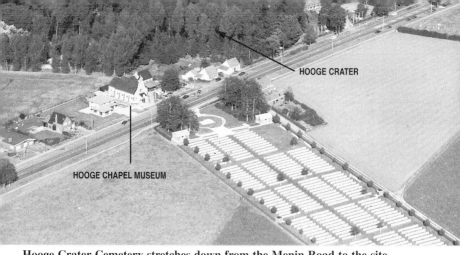

HOOGE CRATER

HOOGE CHAPEL MUSEUM

Hooge Crater Cemetery stretches down from the Menin Road to the site of Zouave Wood.

The cemetery was begun by the 7th Division's burial officer at the beginning of October 1917, when that Division was involved in the fighting near Polygon Wood and made their successful advance to the east and the Broodseinde Ridge. By the time that the war ended there were only 76 graves, to be found in Rows A to D of Plot 1. Over five and a half thousand graves were concentrated here from smaller cemeteries from the battlefields forward of here, mainly from Zillebeke, Zandvoorde and Gheluvelt. The vast majority of those buried here are British; just under ten percent are from Australia. Amongst this latter number is Private Bugden VC, whose grave was brought here from its original position south of Glencorse Wood. Given the circumstances, it is surprising that some 35% of those buried here are actually identified.

MEMORIALS

1. The Fifth (Australian) Memorial

The Australian divisional memorials are scattered across France and Belgium, each division choosing a site that meant most to it. They are to be found, for example, at Pozieres and Riqueval. The Fifth Division's is placed on top of the Butte, which rises some six metres above the cemetery. After the war the Australian government purchased it and German prisoners were set to work on it to produce the elegant shape seen today. By the end of the fighting in October it was a pulverised mess, a process which continued until the spring of 1918, albeit to a lesser degree. It was honeycombed with dugouts, which were refurbished, and were used as brigade and battalion headquarters. On

The 5th Australian Division Memorial stands on top of the Butte, transformed to this shape by German PoWs in 1919.

19 February these dugouts were abandoned, gassed and deliberately collapsed by the New Zealanders who were at the time holding the line.

The Fifth Division suffered its worst casualties, certainly in terms of casualties per day, at Fromelles, a diversionary attack launched on 19 July 1916, which turned out to be a tragic disaster. It performed magnificently at Villers Bretonneux in the spring of 1918. It is understandable why the Butte was chosen, however - for the great pushes beyond Polygon Wood, and subsequently up on to the Broodseinde Ridge were notable and hard fought achievements. It is worth mentioning that the butte was one of the most prominent landmarks in the Salient, visible for miles around, in the period whilst trees and construction did not obstruct the line of sight. It was a very prominent position for the Division's memorial to be placed.

2. The New Zealand Memorial to the Missing, Polygon Wood.

The New Zealand Division moved into this area in November after resting and refitting after their experiences in Third Ypres, where they fought further to the north, to the south west of Passchendaele. They occupied the line from In de Ster Cabaret to the Reutelbeek, On 3 December 1/Canterbury and 1/Otago engaged in an attack to take Polderhoek Chateau, but although they gained ground, the Germans remained in control of the Chateau itself. Soon after the German offensive in March 1918 on the Somme, the great bulk of the Division was transferred there, though it had left this particular sector on 24 February.

> *The dead of the Division in November 1917-February 1918 inclusive, numbered 452, and the missing 89. The names on this Memorial, covering the same period (and excluding the losses of detached units before and after) number 348; of these, 91 belonged to the Canterbury and 127 to the Otago Regiment, the two which attacked Polderhok Chateau. The greater part of the dead fell in the trenches, or in working and carrying; and the conditions in the Salient during the winter of 1917-18 must explain the comparatively large number of names on this Memorial, which deals with only one set attack on an enemy position.*[1]

The Register records particulars of 382 men.

The New Zealand Division is acknowledged by military historians to have been one of the finest fighting formations on the Western Front.

Because the Memorial has the names of so many men of 1/Canterbury (91) and 1/Otago (125) I have included a short account of their attack on Polderhoek Chateau on 3 December here.

Polderhoek Chateau continued to be a thorn in the British side.

> *From it* [the spur] *the enemy not only enfiladed our forward trenches about Cameron Covert and Reutel, but fully commanded and incessantly harassed the whole of our approaches to this sector of our front. On it were perched the piled ruins of Polderhoek Chateau and groups of pillboxes which occupied sites of the attached buildings amid the shattered trees of the once luxuriant and beautiful pleasances. The Ypres Battle had seen three assaults delivered on the spur, and the Chateau had been temporarily won, but only to be lost again to German counter-attacks.*[2]

It was also felt that German fire from the Gheluvelt Plateau would not be nearly so bad or as effective as that which was brought to bear on the British positions by the garrison of Polderhoek Chateau. It would also be a useful means of harassing the enemy and providing a better starting point for any British offensive in the spring of 1918.

An attack from the flank was considered, but the problems of German fire from Becelaere and Juniper Wood, the artillery problems, and the morass of the Reutelbeek, which would have to be crossed, ruled out this option. A frontal attack had the advantage of being launched from trenches directly opposite and close to the Chateau, as well as providing a good barrage line for the artillery. A programme of heavy artillery shelling was followed, beginning on 28 November. Observers 'could see large numbers of Germans rush out of the cellars into the open to escape the concussion caused by our super-heavies' shells'. The attack was to take place on 3 December, to be carried out by 1/Otago and 1/Canterbury. The companies were reduced to 100 all ranks (ie creating a battle reserve thereby).

The selected personnel, who included a large proportion of reinforcements without previous experience of battle, rehearsed the operation behind Ypres on ground laid out to scale, with the buildings and pillboxes numbered as on the map and represented by heaps of material. Parties were also sent up to reconnoitre and observe the ground from the 2nd Canterbury lines and from Cameron Covert.

The attack was to be at noon. The disadvantages of the daylight attack would be negated by the fact that the enemy would not expect it; that they would be taking shelter from the barrage which was customarily being fired at that hour; that smoke would blind the German positions at Becelaere and on the Gheluvelt Spur, and these latter positions would be covered with a heavy artillery barrage, accompanied by a machine-gun barrage and gas. Positions in the Chateau and its grounds would be covered by machine-guns barrages, and the new 6 inch medium trench mortars were positioned in Reutel to neutralise, by gas shells, machine-guns in and around Juniper Wood.

An immediate preliminary bombardment might, on account of their proximity to the targets, be dangerous to the congested troops in our line, and at the same time would reduce the potent effect of surprise. It was therefore dispensed with. At one and the same moment the barrage guns would open and the infantry would rush to the assault.

1/Otago would be on the left; the Chateau lay within their boundary.. 1/Canterbury would be on the right, but faced the problems of a series of strong pill boxes including those at the stables and the Manager's house (itself supposedly connected to the Chateau by a tunnel). 1/Canterbury would form a defensive flank on its south from the

View from approximate site of the British Front Line to the west of Polderhoek Chateau.

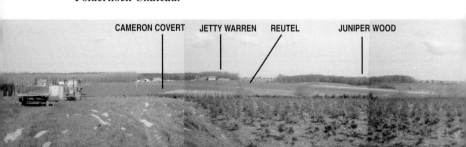

CAMERON COVERT   JETTY WARREN   REUTEL   JUNIPER WOOD

outset, facing the Gheluvelt Spur. The battalions would advance with a company each abreast, with a second company each fifty yards behind. The first wave would carry the line to the intermediate objective beyond the objective; the second wave would carry the line on some three hundred yards, providing observation to the ground beyond. The support companies would move into the old front line positions once they were cleared, to hold them in case of counter-attacks, and the reserve companies would be kept in the rear, ready to move up and occupy the final line, relieving the assaulting troops.

The attack was launched, and one battery of artillery fired short, causing casualties to the left of 1/Otago.

Undismayed, however, the first wave pushed on, crossed our front line and were rapidly among the wilderness of tree-stumps where the wire was found demolished. Our hopes of catching the enemy off his guard were doomed to disappointment. The fear of our heavies' daily forenoon bombardment had not driven the garrison into underground refuge. His pillboxes were occupied as usual, and his sentries were normally vigilant. Almost as soon as our artillery opened, his machine-guns cracked vociferously, both from the pillboxes about the Chateau and from the Gheluvelt Ridge. A few moments later his artillery put down an intense barrage on the duck-board track and about Veldhoek....

1/Canterbury came under fire from pillboxes and by fire from Gheluvelt

for in that direction our plans had miscarried. A strong west wind dissipated and rendered useless our protective smoke barrage and all our artillery activity was powerless to subdue the well-posted and well-protected Gheluvelt machine-guns.

It was whilst dealing with a German strong point and gun that Private Henry Nicholas of 1/Canterbury won the VC. He killed twelve Germans with rifle, bayonet and grenades and wounded the remaining four members of the garrison. He was to be killed the following year, at the end of October 1918. Further stubborn resistance, centred on pillboxes, brought the attack on the right to a stumbling halt, and they ended up some 150 yards

BECELAERE CHURCH   POLDERHOEK CHATEAU

short of the first objective. 1/Otago was held up by an overwhelming barrage of fire from the Chateau, so that they too were forced to dig in on the same line as 1/Canterbury. Some men had indeed managed to work round beyond the flank of the Chateau ruins, but were blown away by enemy artillery or by heavy machine-gun fire from fortified shell holes or from a sixty yard length of trench that was to the left rear of the Chateau.[3]

The attack had failed, but the consolation prize was that full command had been gained of the ground in the Scherriabeek valley, the stream that formed the valley to the south of the Polderhoek Spur. Its importance was illustrated by the repeated attempts made by the Germans to regain this ground over the next couple of days, all of which attempts were seen off with the enemy suffering heavy casualties.

Most of the ground was lost in a German attack on 10 December, after the New Zealanders had returned to their sector, to the immediate north of the Reutelbeek. The casualties were heavy; as stated above, this is reflected in the large numbers of men whose name are recorded on the Memorial at Polygon Wood.

Short Tour to Polderhoek Chateau.

A tour of the Polderhoek Chateau attack may be made, although the motorway has changed matters considerably, in particular to the ground to the rear of the New Zealand jump off line and the ground to **Polderhoek Chateau taken before the war.**

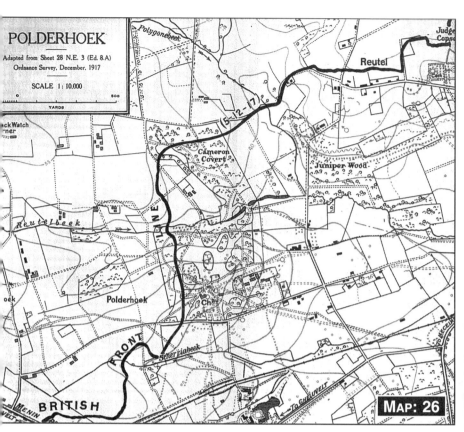

MAP: 26

The photograph shows what remained of Polderhoek Chateau in October 1917.

the south. Drive past Juniper Wood and take the first turning right. The road is not good quality and is a cul de sac. After about five hundred yards a track leads off to the right up to a farm which is situated on the site of parts of the Chateau. Carry on along the road for about a hundred yards and this is (approximately) a point on the line, running north and south from here, that was taken. It is probably worth while getting out and peering down to the south east to get an idea of what sort of view this gave; to the south west you will be confronted by the motorway. Proceed along the road, continuing on it as it bends to the right and runs parallel with the motorway, stopping before the farm house at the end of the road on a patch of hard ground where you can turn around. This is a little behind the New Zealand start line, but walk forward to the eastern edge of the hard ground and you can see down into the Reutelbeek valley and get some idea of the problems facing 1/Otago.

1. Memorial Register 8. *The Buttes New British Cemetery (New Zealand) Memorial, Polygon Wood, Zonnebeke,* (Imperial War Graves Commission, London, 1927) p. 6

2. Colonel H Stewart, *The New Zealand Division 1916 - 1919,* Whitcombe and Tombs Ltd, Auckland, 1921. Much of my account is drawn from this history, in particular pp 304-314.

3. Lieutenant AE Byrne MC, *Official History of the Otago Regiment, NZEF, in the Great War 1914 - 1918,* J Wilkie and Co, Dunedin n.d. pp 230 -239. There is also a lengthy, and intelligent, analysis of what went wrong with the attack and wider lessons that could be learned - too much to include in this book.

INDEX